This book is dedicated to all the

teachers, students and loved ones

who helped me succeed in, survive and enjoy

my first teaching job.

Contents

Acknowledgements

Special thanks go to all the staff who worked with me at Drayton Manor High School, especially John Rust-Andrews, Linda Huntley, John Browning, David Henderson, Simon Horne, Caroline Evernden, Luan Binnion, Jenny Burn, Chris Everall and Kate McClean. Thanks also to all my teachers at Kingston University and to my publishers, Bloomsbury. Extra special thanks and love go to my Mum and to Tilak, Álvie and Edite.

Preface to the third edition

I'm delighted to be updating this book, which I originally wrote just after leaving my first teaching post. Even all these years on, my memories of my own newly qualified year are vivid and rather magical. Some of the friendships I made in my first school survive to this day, even though we have all moved on a great deal since then (and gained a fair few wrinkles/pounds/children in the intervening years). Some of the older teachers I worked with are long since retired, or have moved on to the great staffroom in the sky, where perhaps they can finally put their feet up and actually finish that cup of tea. Some of the younger teachers I worked with are now in senior management roles, a few even making it to the dizzy heights of headship. Occasionally a student from my early days gets in touch to tell me about how he or she is progressing in the adult world. How lucky you are to be taking your own first steps on that same wonderful journey.

In this brand new edition of *How to Survive your First Year in Teaching* you'll find lots of tips and suggestions that I have collected since I first wrote the book. Some are ideas that I picked up as I moved on to work in different kinds of schools, with different types of children, in new kinds of situations. Others I have gathered through my training work with students, NQTs, teachers and support staff in schools and colleges around the UK and in Europe as well. All the time on my travels, I am picking up valuable suggestions that should make life in the classroom better and easier for you. I've crammed as many of these strategies as I can fit into this new edition.

Although I've freshened things up and brought this book up to date, what I haven't done is completely rewrite it, because I wanted to retain the essential flavour of how it felt to be new to the job. The excitement and apprehension of setting foot in the classroom as a 'proper' teacher for the very first time. The ins and outs of the working life of a teacher. All the ups and downs, and the sheer *reality* of what the job involves.

Things change all the time in teaching, particularly where they concern newly qualified teachers. Since I originally qualified, a vast number of new initiatives and acronyms have come into play (TAs, QTS, IWBs, DfE, School Direct, academies and 'free' schools to name just a few). Similarly today's new teachers are expected to jump through far more hoops than used to be the case. While this book will guide you on the most painless route through that maze of acronyms and government requirements, it is at heart a book about the *practicalities* of coming into the profession and of becoming an effective teacher. What you'll soon discover is that these things remain pretty much timeless, whoever is in charge and whatever the current buzzwords or hot topics might be.

I do hope this book helps you as you set out on the journey to becoming a qualified teacher; the same journey that I made all those years ago. It's a fantastic trip, and it will take you to places that you could never have imagined. It will be tough, it will be fun, it will be stressful, it will be joyful. But one thing is for sure: it will never ever be dull.

Sue Cowley
www.suecowley.co.uk

Introduction

You've worked long and hard to qualify as a teacher; after plenty of form filling and some nerve racking interviews you've found yourself a job; and now it's time to put it all into practice. But how ready do you feel to stand in front of a class and teach? And how do you deal with all the other important parts of a teaching job? Somehow, that's something they forgot to tell you at university. Don't panic though, because this book will help you understand all these things and much much more.

When I started teaching I was amazed to find out how inefficient schools can be: how much time is wasted on inessential tasks; how disciplined you have to be to spend your time effectively; how often inadequate systems and ineffective management can add stress to your working life. I was also surprised to discover that a few simple but effective strategies could make a huge difference to my chances of success as a teacher. Many of these techniques were picked up from experienced teachers; others I simply worked out for myself.

In teaching you are your own boss (mostly), and this is one of the joys of working in the profession. But the job expands to meet the amount of time you are willing to devote to it. As a new teacher you are full of energy and enthusiasm, but you must develop self-discipline and time management skills if you're going to avoid working until midnight every night. There are so many things about teaching that are learnt on the job, during that challenging first couple of years. You will need to find ways to deal with problem students and awkward parents; to decide how much time you can afford to spend on marking; and to develop a teaching style that works for you. This book will assist you in your quest to develop into the best teacher you can possibly be, while also keeping yourself healthy, happy and sane.

I can remember feeling at sea during my first year of teaching, adrift without any certainties to anchor on to, drowning in a sea of paperwork.

This book contains answers to all the questions I had and gives you realistic guidance in overcoming the obstacles that confront you. This is *not* an academic textbook based on years of painstaking research. It is a book of common-sense advice, based on my own experiences in schools, and all that I have learnt from other teachers. I have combined practical tips and suggestions with examples (often light-hearted) to help you as you start out on your teaching career. As the saying goes, it's not rocket science. We're talking common sense – these are mostly things you'll work out for yourself when you get them wrong. My aim is to help you avoid making those painful mistakes in the first place.

These days, there are many different routes into teaching. This book is aimed at all those who are just starting out in the profession, whether you're a newly qualified teacher, on the Teach First or School Direct Training Programme, doing a school centered training course, or a trainee teacher on a PGCE or similar qualification. I've been lucky enough to teach at nursery, primary, secondary and post compulsory levels, in the UK and also overseas. And what I've realised is how similar students are, whatever their age and wherever they live. So many of the techniques I use with three-year-olds are applicable to teenagers and adults as well; so many of the challenges that face the primary teacher are the same for teachers in the secondary sector. This book is aimed at *all* teachers, whatever age group and wherever you teach.

I'd like to wish you luck in your prospective profession – you have chosen one of the most varied, interesting and rewarding jobs it is possible to find. You have also chosen a career that is exhausting, incredibly hard work and which may sometimes reduce you to tears. The thing to hold onto, though, during the tough first year, is that you can make a real and genuine difference to your children's lives. And at some point in the future they may look back and remember you as someone who really mattered to them. What other career could offer such a wonderful reward?

PART I

Getting Started

Chapter 1
Survival tactics

What is this chapter about?

Much of the time, teaching is a wonderful and fulfilling job. There will be moments during your first year though, when it feels more like a case of day to day survival. There's a very steep learning curve during your first few years as a teacher, but hold onto the thought that it does get easier with time and experience. Once you are established within your role, and have spent a year or so at your school, everything will start to slot into place. This first chapter will help you survive through the tricky early part of your career, and especially during your first year.

Before you start

The months and weeks before you start your first teaching job are an exciting but nervous time. Your mind will be full of a combination of questions that you want answered, ideas about lessons you could do with your children, and worries about issues such as managing behaviour. Here are a few quick tips to help you cope at this stage:

Go easy on the planning
Do not succumb to the overwhelming temptation to spend the summer planning loads of wonderful and exciting schemes of work. Although you may believe that you are saving yourself time, any detailed or in-depth planning done at this stage is pretty pointless. Until you meet your students

and get to know them a little, it is hard to anticipate their needs and interests. It is also likely that much of your teaching will be based on schemes of work or textbooks already in use at your school. If you get the chance to visit your school before you start work, ask about how planning works and whether anything can be done in advance.

Stock up on the fun stuff

What is helpful is to hunt around for some cheap or free bits and bobs that will be useful, perhaps in lessons or maybe as part of a reward system. Keep an eye out for giveaways, promotional offers, and in charity shops. Look for unusual, eye-catching and inspirational resources. Some of the very best are completely free – an empty bird's nest, a skeleton leaf, an unusual pebble. Scan the internet too for interesting ideas and useful links.

Fit in a visit

If you get the chance, visit your new school during the summer term. Although they will have shown you around on the day of the interview, you were probably feeling too tense to take much in. If no one offers a visit, contact the school and ask whether it would be possible. During your visit, get a feel for how the classrooms look, spend time looking at your space if you can, and consider whether you'd like to rearrange the furniture. If possible, ask to meet some of your children and to sit in on some lessons. This will give you a 'feel' for what they are going to be like to teach.

Arrange a mooting with important people

During your visit it's useful to have a quick chat with those people who are going to be important during your induction year. This might not be possible, or it might simply be a quick 'hello/goodbye' – schools are very busy places. Your list of 'important people' could include:

- your induction mentor
- the teacher of the year group you will be teaching (primary)
- the key stage coordinator of the year group you will be teaching (primary)
- the teacher of the class you will be teaching (primary)
- any TAs (teaching assistants) or support staff you will be working with

- your head of department or faculty (secondary)
- your head of house or year group (secondary)
- the SENCO (Special Educational Needs Co-ordinator).

Make the most of your holiday

The best advice of all is to take a long and relaxing holiday before you plunge into the stressful world of the full-time teacher. Whether your finances will be up to this is another matter.

The first day

In reality you will have two 'first' days. There will be one or more in-service training (INSET) days before the children return to school; this will be followed by the actual start of term, when the students arrive back.

The INSET day

Your first INSET day may feel rather intimidating. The staff will be gathered in the staffroom, chatting away to each other, discussing all the exciting things they did over the summer. You will probably only know a couple of people from the day of your interview. These ideas and tips should help you get through the day:

Don't dress too smartly

In most cases it is acceptable to dress casually for training days, although if you feel unsure about doing this you could wear smart casual clothing. The discomfort of being in a suit when everyone else is in jeans is something you could do without at this stage.

Be prepared for meetings

Training days are typically busy with meetings. Your day might start with a full staff meeting, at which the head will welcome everyone back, explain any promotions that have taken place and introduce the new teachers (including you). Warning: they will probably ask you to stand up when you are welcomed to the school. There could be various administrative and whole-school issues to deal with, for instance if your school is due for an inspection or is re-vamping policies. In a secondary school you will probably have to attend a departmental or pastoral meeting as well.

Be prepared for admin
There will also be lots of administration tasks to do – sorting books and resources, labelling books, checking deliveries and so on. These tasks eat up a surprisingly large amount of time.

Be prepared for training
Many schools use one of the September INSET days to do some whole-staff training. As you progress in your career, you'll find that the training you receive is of variable usefulness, depending mostly on the quality of the trainer. If you're lucky, you will get some great ideas and tips; if you're unlucky, you will get 'death by PowerPoint'.

Use preparation time wisely
Preparation time gives you the opportunity to get to know other members of your department or teachers working in classrooms close to your own, or in your key stage. Take care with first impressions: even if you are the most confident individual in the world, keep fairly quiet at this stage to avoid making the wrong impression.

Don't get too organised too soon
When you receive that pile of key papers on the INSET day, it is very tempting to start organising them immediately: sticking your timetable and class lists into your planner, writing out your first week's lessons, and so on. Avoid this temptation. The first week of school never runs quite according to the timetable – for instance on the first day back the students may have assemblies and extra registration or tutor time. Class lists, too, are often subject to change when new children join the school or others do not turn up. Keep all your important papers in a folder to deal with at a later stage.

Personalise your room
The majority of teachers will get a 'room of their own', and now is the time to stamp your personality on your room. (Although it is worth noting that some secondary schools lack space, and you may be forced to move around from classroom to classroom for different lessons.) If you do get your own

room, ensure that the students get the impression that it is your territory, and that you are well prepared and well organised. You could:

- put up a 'Welcome' sign with your name on your door
- add some colourful posters to the walls, and put up some key word displays
- create a chart or display for your rewards and sanctions systems
- rearrange the seating if you think it would work better in another configuration
- organise and label trays or drawers (add pictures if you are working with young children)
- sift through the drawer in your desk and clear out the debris left by last year's class teacher.

Get your bearings

One of the main difficulties you will face at first is finding your way around the school buildings, especially in a large secondary school. Get hold of a map and study it closely, highlighting the important places. Then spend some time walking around the place, preferably with someone who is familiar with it. Your children may also be new to the school, and will need you to help them find *their* way around! Make sure you know the location of:

- the school office
- the student reception
- the head's office
- the deputy head's office
- the offices of senior staff, e.g. assistant head teachers, heads of year
- the photocopier
- the admin staff
- the assembly hall
- the canteen
- the staffroom
- the student toilets
- the staff toilets.

Collecting resources

This is also the time to get hold of all the resources you are likely to need in your first few weeks. Everyone else will be grabbing theirs, and vital resources can become like gold dust as the term goes on. If you're not sure where to find these things, grab your mentor and don't let go until he/she tells you! Use the checklist below to ensure that you have everything you need before your children arrive.

Resources Checklist	Tick
A teacher's planner (a diary, with sections for planning, marking, class lists, etc.)	
Passwords or log-in details to access the school's computer systems	
A finalised copy of your timetable	
Your class list or lists	
Details of any children in your class who have special educational needs or disabilities	
Information about individual plans/strategies for these children	
Planning formats for your lesson planning	
Schemes of work, short and medium term plans	
Exam syllabus for GCSE classes	
Set of whole-school policies (as a priority get hold of and read the behaviour policy)	
Resources for rewards and sanctions systems – merit stamp, stickers, certificates, pro forma letters to send home, etc.	
Class sets of books or textbooks	
Materials for artwork and displays	
Exercise books, homework diaries	
Variety of types of paper – plain, scrap, lined, graph, sugar	
Pens, pencils, rubbers	

Resources Checklist	Tick
Paper clips, bulldog clips	
Staplers and staples, staple gun (for displays) and staples	
Scissors	
Rulers	
Glue sticks and sellotape	
Blu-tack or pins	
Mini whiteboards	
Whiteboard markers, permanent markers	
Laminator and laminating pouches	
Coloured pens and pencils	
Tutor group diaries and timetables (for tutors in a secondary school)	

The first lesson

So here it is at last, the moment you've been waiting for. Your stomach feels like lead, you're convinced you are going to be sick and your mouth is as dry as the Sahara desert. Even experienced teachers find the start of term difficult; how on earth are you supposed to cope with it?

At this point I'd like to offer you a few brief thoughts to help you survive this nerve racking experience:

You are 'the mystery teacher'

No one knows who you are yet. Your children may suspect that you are inexperienced, but unless you tell them, or give that impression, they have no way of knowing for sure. At the moment you are an unknown quantity and consequently you have an air of mystery that you can exploit. If a student asks 'Are you a new teacher, Miss/Sir?' you might answer, 'Just new to this school'. Cultivate the sense that you have a wealth of experience behind you, teaching or otherwise. No matter how inexperienced *you* are, the students will always be younger and less experienced.

'They're more scared of you...'

You know the old saying about spiders and snakes: *'They're more scared of you than you are of them'*? This saying also holds true for your children. Most students will give you a window of opportunity in which to prove yourself; a few lessons during which they are checking you out, unsure about how far they can push you.

Just as when you are dealing with a nervous animal, the key is to appear relaxed. If you look calm, confident and in control of yourself, the children will probably behave fine for you. If you get flustered, defensive or aggressive, they may strike out.

Have a sense of style

Think about your teaching style before your first lesson. The old cliché contains a lot of truth: *'Start off as hard as possible – you can always relax, but you can never get a class back once you've lost them.'* You are not their friend, mother/father figure or counsellor, you are their teacher. Your students will expect and indeed *want* a degree of formality from you. I'm not suggesting that you scare the living daylights out of them, but be as firm as you can manage. Once you get to know your children during the year, you may be able to relax. If you start soft you are laying down trouble for yourself in the future. Honestly.

While we're on the subject of clichés, let's deal with that other favourite adage: *'Don't smile before Christmas.'* Essentially, this is a metaphor rather than something to be taken literally. There's absolutely no harm in smiling at your children, but just make sure it's an *'I'm in charge'* kind of smile, rather than an *'I'll roll over and do whatever you want'* one.

Relax

It's important, for your own sake and for that of the children, not to rush your first few lessons. Try to relax and don't worry if there are brief pauses while you consider what you want to do next. If your mind does go blank, look around the class with a confident air, making eye contact with some individuals. After a while it will all come easily, I promise.

You'll find lots of hints on managing behaviour and learning in Chapters 3 and 4, but for now, to help ensure that you have a successful first lesson, on the next few pages are some of my top tips for classroom and behaviour management.

1. Set the boundaries now

In the first lesson, the name of the game is boundary setting: *'this is what I expect from you, this is why I expect it, this is what will happen if you do or do not follow the rules'*. Your boundaries should be fair, realistic and achievable, focusing on positive rather than negative behaviour. Once you've set your boundaries, stick to them like glue. Talk with the class about the behaviour you need and why you need it, and if appropriate let them give their own ideas. That way, your children will feel secure about how they should behave and you can get on with the teaching. If you fail to set clear boundaries, or if you constantly move the goalposts, the students will mess you around to see how far they can push you.

Your school will have a set of classroom rules as part of its behaviour policy – use these as your starting point. School rules work well so long as they are realistic, appropriate to the students, and applied consistently by all staff. Problems can arise if staff are inconsistent in applying the rules, if the rules are too vague, or if they are hopelessly unrealistic for dealing with really confrontational students.

The way that you set and maintain boundaries is a matter of personal taste – it's about establishing the teaching style you want to use. It also depends on the age and type of your students – it will vary if you're working with Year 1 or Year 6, or with Year 7 or Year 11. After a while you will work out how best to establish your expectations with different classes. In Chapter 3 you'll find some examples of boundaries, sanctions and rewards you could set for a class in the first lesson.

2. Wait for them

I cover this idea in more detail later on, but it bears repeating a million times. It is certainly never more important than in your first meeting with the students. Even the proverbial 'class from hell' should hopefully listen to you the first time they meet you. Set the standard now, so they know what you expect. Keep this maxim in mind: *Never talk to a class until every single student is sitting still, in complete silence, looking directly at you.* Or, to put it another way, *One person speaks at a time.* As well as insisting that the students listen in silence to you, insist that they listen in silence to each other – it's only right and respectful. Set this pattern of behaviour now and I promise you that you won't regret it. It will probably be difficult to achieve, but it is the cornerstone of effective learning.

Having silent attention allows the teacher to get on with teaching, and the children to get on with learning. It tells your class that their learning is important, and that you will try your hardest to ensure that they are not disrupted. If you don't wait for complete silence, at first you might only be talking over low level chatter from one or two students, but it's a slippery slope – after a while you will find it impossible to get *anyone* to listen.

In some really challenging schools, you may have difficulty gaining the class's attention, even in the first lesson. If this happens, don't panic. Have some back up strategies in your mind that you can use if the class won't listen. In Chapter 3 you'll find lots of suggestions to try if getting silent attention is tricky for you to achieve.

3. Hands up!

A big irritant in the classroom is when children call out their answers during Q&A sessions. Get your students into good habits right from the word go, by starting questions with the phrase, *'Put your hand up if you can tell me...'*. After a while you will have trained your children to respond to every question by raising their hands. You can introduce alternatives to hands up, such as names on a lolly stick, as you get to know your class.

4. Admin, admin, admin, names

There are lots of administrative tasks to complete in the first few lessons with any class. Checking registers, explaining rules, giving out books all takes time. Don't feel that you have to rush into delivering the curriculum. Have as your key focus getting to know the students and learning a few names, perhaps by playing some name games.

5. Use the register

I've always found taking the register is a good way to start lessons in the secondary school – it helps to settle the class down and it sends a message about your teaching style. In a primary class it is of course a vital task at the beginning of the day. At secondary level, get into the habit of taking the register in every lesson you teach. When you come to write reports, you need to know about student attendance levels. The register can also be used to check who owes homework and keep an eye on any students who might be late to lessons or truanting from them.

6. Who wants a job?

Whenever you have anything to be given out or collected in, ask this question of the class. You will find that your students are delighted to help you (especially the younger ones) and you will save yourself unnecessary work. Use the offer of a job as a reward for keen students.

7. Stand behind your chairs

This is a worthwhile (and very simple) strategy which helps you control your class and also saves you time and effort. At the end of the lesson or the day, just before the bell goes, ask your children to stand behind their chairs (or place the chairs on desks) and wait to be dismissed. You then have the students' attention for giving out any instructions or reminders, you can walk around and check that there is no litter on the floor, and you have saved yourself the job of pushing in the chairs. Once you have set this pattern, you will find that the students stand behind their chairs automatically.

An extension of this idea is to turn the exercise into a 'game' for younger children. Tell them that they are being 'tested' on how quietly they can stand behind their chairs. This makes the end of the lesson nice and restful for you, as it avoids scraping chairs (and much quieter for the teacher of the class below you if you are on the first floor). A further extension is to tell the children they must freeze like statues until the bell goes, giving out rewards for this to encourage them.

The first week

By the end of the first week you should be finding your feet. If you are a primary teacher, you will know your children reasonably well by this stage. If you work at secondary level, you should have faced each of your classes at least once. You will also have an idea of what your timetable is like and the structure of your days. At this stage, there are a few things that you can do to prepare yourself for the weeks and months to come:

- *Get an overview:* Get a sense of the balance of your days and weeks. Perhaps your mornings are very intensive in terms of teacher input, with primary literacy and numeracy lessons. At secondary level, there may be days when all your classes are difficult to control, but other days when you teach only well behaved students.

- *Plan for a balanced approach:* When you've gained this overview of your week, try and account for it in your planning. Don't plan whole days of lessons that require lots of teacher input and talking, as this will put a strain on your voice. If you have to face a series of classes with difficult students, try to incorporate some lessons that lessen the stress, for instance visiting the library or watching a learning related film.

- *Keep an eye on your marking load:* Some subjects, topics or lessons create huge piles of marking, while others mean a relatively light marking load. Achieve a balance in your marking as well as in your planning. Keep an eye on the type of tasks you are setting and don't set too much work that requires detailed marking at any one time. Incorporate plenty of oral, practical and student-led activities, as these are generally less time-consuming to assess.

Developing support systems

Whatever job you do it is important to have someone to turn to for help: a shoulder to cry on when things are going wrong; someone to ask when you need advice or information. In teaching these support systems are absolutely vital. Teaching is a very difficult job and you will be put in situations where you are challenged in many different ways: physically, emotionally, psycho-logically and even legally.

Develop your support systems as soon as possible, preferably *before* you have to use them. Support systems come in a variety of forms – the one you need to use will depend on the type of problem you are experiencing.

Your teaching colleagues

In schools there are surprisingly few chances to meet with other teachers, particularly if you are working in a large school. You might have some contact with those who work in classrooms close to your own, or with other members of your department, but the majority of each day will be spent with your students. Although it can seem a lot of hassle to get to the staffroom, it's worth making the effort. You get the chance to chat with other teachers and you also give yourself a break from the children.

As soon as possible, get involved in any social activities that are taking place (a staff game of football or netball, going out for a drink). One of the best resources in any school is its staff and their experience. Your teaching colleagues can give you many things: advice, information, schemes of work, a chance to moan or to cry on a sympathetic shoulder.

Your induction mentor

As a newly qualified teacher you will have an induction tutor or mentor – an experienced teacher who will guide you through your first year, watching you at work, assessing your progress, and checking to see whether you meet the induction standards. Your mentor will become a vital part of your support system, particularly if you find that you get on well together. More information about induction can be found in Chapter 12.

Support staff

There are a range of back-up staff who play a vital part in supporting teachers. You might have the help of a TA or LSA, the services of a technician, or the assistance of a special needs teacher in your lessons. Make some time early on to sit down with your support staff to discuss how best you can work together, drawing on the experience and expertise of those people who work with and alongside you. These staff can offer you invaluable assistance in developing your planning and teaching to suit the children, and give you insights into different characters in your class.

Your head of department

In the secondary school, the head of department or faculty is responsible for all the members of staff in a particular area. This person also has responsibility for what is taught and how it is delivered. He or she will also deal with any parent or student comments (good or bad) about your work. It is a excellent idea, both on a professional and a personal level, to develop a good working relationship with your head of department. An effective head of department will support you in times of need and will also help you to develop your career.

Non-teaching members of staff

There are a lot of people working in schools who are not part of the teaching staff: caretakers, receptionists, secretaries, bursars, photocopying assistants, and so on. These people can support you in many different ways, so take the time to get to know them. They might help you in arranging a trip; moving furniture at short notice; accessing computerised information; typing letters, and so on.

Teaching unions

While there is no compulsion for teachers to join a union, there are many advantages in doing so, and a union can form a vital part of your support system. An important advantage of belonging to a union is the technical advice and support on legal and contractual issues that they offer. With all the stresses of starting work as a teacher, it is very helpful to gain straight-forward advice on such matters. As a new member of staff you may feel uncomfortable approaching a more senior teacher with these questions; a union representative can offer you non-partisan advice. The unions also offer good training events and obviously they stand up for teachers' rights in negotiations about pay and conditions. Most unions offer some type of discount for membership in your trainee and NQT years.

The first term: September to December

Your first term at school will be a busy and exciting time. As you get to know the students and find your way around the buildings you will start to grow in confidence. Half-term will seem to arrive very quickly and your workload may even seem manageable. This term is full of fun and excitement in the build-up to Christmas: there will be lots of events going on and you should really be able to enjoy yourself. There are, however, a few factors to be aware of at this stage:

- *Overconfidence:* Take care that you don't become overconfident and consequently relax with your classes too early. Your students may be responding well to the boundaries that you have set, but if you allow your standards to slip they could quickly lapse into poor behaviour. An air of over excitement can develop in schools as the winter holiday approaches. Remember though, that you will have to face your children again after Christmas. Come January, the end of the school year suddenly seems very far away.

- *Extra activities:* Be careful about getting involved with lots of extra activities: the Christmas concert, the school play, working parties, the Parent-Teacher Association (PTA) and so on. It is very tempting when you start teaching to join in with anything and everything to make a good impression. More experienced members of staff will have learned how to refuse excessive demands on their time. You might find it hard to refuse if someone asks you to help out. Ensure that teaching and learning remain your top priority.

- *Illness/exhaustion/stress:* You want to keep going, to prove to your school that you are a reliable, hard-working employee. So, when you catch flu you muddle through and then you wonder why you can't shift the succession of colds that follow. Teachers are notorious for going to work when they should be at home in bed with a lemsip. *'My classes need me'*, they say, *'I'll only have twice as much work to do when I get back.'* A lot of teachers keep going and going and then every holiday, without fail, they fall ill.

    A few points for you to think about: are you really so irreplaceable that the school cannot do without you for one or two days? Do you really want to pass on the flu to all the other staff? And isn't it better to take a day off now and then when you need it, rather than two weeks off when you finally realise that you just can't keep going any longer?

    When you need to take time off sick, follow the school policy on absence. This will probably involve phoning your school to notify them that you will be away, the reason for your absence, and your likely return date. You may have to phone in for each day you are sick. You will need to set work, and you may have to 'sign in' on the day you return to school, registering your return with the school office.

- *Evaluation:* As an NQT your progress will be officially evaluated and some of your lessons will be appraised. Chapter 12 provides more information about the induction process. Get into the habit of doing informal self-evaluations, to prepare yourself for observations – it's one of the best, quickest and easiest ways of improving your teaching. If one of your lessons goes particularly well, take a few minutes to think about what made it good, so that you can repeat your success in the future. Similarly, if you use a teaching strategy that doesn't work, or if you get into a confrontation, think about why the problem occurred and how you can prevent it happening again in the future.

The second term: January to April

Any teacher will tell you that the second term of the school year is the hardest. The days are cold and dark, with limited hours of daylight. The staff are tired and run-down, and waves of illness spread through the school like wildfire, hitting teachers and children. Spring and summer seem an age away and the rest of the school year stretches ahead of you like a prison sentence. You have the mother of all hangovers from Christmas and the New Year. The paperwork is starting to pile up and you're wondering whether you made the wrong career choice. Here are a few tips for getting through your second term:

- *Plan a half-term holiday:* An excellent way of beating the second term blues is to go on holiday in the February half-term. Don't take any work with you, escape somewhere relaxing and warm, and impress your students by sending them an exotic postcard. If you stay at home, try not to work all through the break. Plan a series of fun days out to pamper and reinvigorate yourself.

- *Reclaim your spare time:* If you got involved in extra curricular activities during the first term (for instance the Christmas play), you should find that you get your evenings back now. While you might use spare time after school for work, far better to devote it to yourself instead, for instance by taking up a physical or creative activity.

- *Experiment!:* Now is a good time to take a few risks in your lessons: to plan a few unusual activities and see how they work. By this stage, you should hopefully have developed a good relationship with your children. Although I would still warn against relaxing too early, there is certainly the opportunity to experiment a little in your lesson content and delivery in the second term.

The third term: May to July

At last! The end of your first year is in sight. The third term always comes as a relief and is often a very enjoyable time. Examinations will be taking place, and some secondary students might be on study leave, giving you some free lessons. Although your marking load could become quite heavy, you will be amazed at how the word 'exam' turns your children into silent and hard-working young people. Here are some thoughts and tips for the summer term:

- *Enjoy it:* Now is the time to relax and enjoy your teaching. By this stage your relationship with your students will be clear: you will know who needs firm handling, and who benefits from a more flexible approach. In the summer term you can start to relax a little and enjoy your teaching and your children.

- *Use your time wisely:* It is rare to have any spare time in teaching, so when you do get non-contact time, think carefully about how best to use it. Yes, you could spend the time planning, but sometimes just sitting and chatting in the staffroom with some mates is the best use of a free hour. Alternatively, perhaps doing filing and paperwork will give you a sense of achievement.

- *Look for the best:* One of the key ingredients of a successful teacher is the ability to remain positive – to see the best in every child. A lot of schools have their sports day during the summer term, and it can be very enlightening to see some of your most difficult students achieving excellent results on the sports field. Keep an eye open during this term for different types of achievement to note and praise.

- *Beware of the weather:* A word of warning about the summer term: hot weather creates a sense of lethargy, both in teachers and in students. It's up to you whether you decide to crack the whip, or (if you're allowed) to do lots of learning outdoors.

Chapter 2
Planning

What is this chapter about?

Planning as a student and planning as a teacher are two very different things. The same applies to planning for an observation, and planning for your day to day teaching. In each case, the former is at least partly for show, while the latter is about what actually works in your classroom. The difficulty during your first year as a teacher is working out how to plan in a way that is helpful for you and your students, but not too time-consuming. Planning, just like teaching and marking, is a very individual process. What works for one person may be completely unusable for another. In your first year you will probably err on the side of caution, and plan in more detail than is strictly necessary. These detailed plans will not be wasted, though, as you should be able to reuse them in future years. This chapter gives you lots of thoughts, hints and tips about how to start developing your own style of planning, one that really is effective for you.

What is good planning?

Essentially, planning is only effective if it actually works for the individual teacher within his or her classroom. The most vital component of a good plan is that it leads to a high quality lesson, in which effective learning takes place. As a new teacher, the planning process will also help you think through the lesson ahead of time. What you need to develop is the ability to figure out how well the activities within the lesson will work, *before you actually teach it.*

At university, you were probably encouraged to start your planning from the question – 'what do I want the children to learn?'. You can find lots more about learning intentions/outcomes, WALT/WILF, success criteria, aims, objectives, etc. in Chapter 4. Certainly, it's important to think ahead of time about what you're trying to get across to the children, whether it's information, facts, skills, or whatever. But when it comes to planning, life has a habit of getting in the way. It could be that the children do not actually learn what you had originally intended, but that nevertheless they learned a great deal. Or that you simply didn't manage to get through everything you had planned to include within a lesson. Don't worry when this happens, it is all part of the learning process of becoming a teacher and understanding what works for you.

The diagram below gives you an 'at a glance' view on what makes a good plan and the notes that follow describe each part in more detail.

A good lesson plan...
is Balanced

Finding a sense of balance in your planning is tricky and will take a while to get right. Balance comes in two forms: firstly, there should be a balance in your working life between the time spent on planning and on other important parts of the job. Don't spend too much time on lesson planning. If only it were as easy to follow this piece of advice as it is to say it. First, you need to work out what constitutes 'too much time' from your perspective. Your first year will be busy, and your top priority should be what goes on in the classroom. Planning is a key part of this, and you will need to devote a fair amount of time to getting lesson plans right. The secret is not to go overboard or to plan in excessive or superfluous detail.

The second form of balance is that there should be a balance of activities within the lessons themselves. For more on balanced lesson planning, see the next section.

is Engaging

One of the most vital qualities of a good teacher is that he or she is able to engage the children in their learning. A large part of this engagement is to do with planning appropriate, interesting, imaginative and creative tasks for your students. Although you may often feel constrained by the demands of the curriculum, strive to make your lessons as exciting and engaging as possible, as much of the time as is feasible.

has a Clear Objective

Aim to be clear in your mind about what you are specifically hoping the children will learn. At the same time, though, don't close off the options for other exciting possibilities that crop up. Where appropriate, allow your children to move off on tangents if they have a question that they want answered or if you spot a good opportunity to introduce a new idea.

is Easy to Use

A plan is only useful if you can actually use it during the lesson. This is why too much detail can actually be a bad thing – if you find it impossible to refer to the plan quickly and easily, it will tend to stultify rather than aid your teaching. At the same time, your plan must give sufficient detail to make you feel confident about teaching the lesson.

is Reusable

Some teachers plan in lots of detail, others prefer to work from a brief outline. In the 'old days' we might have entered the classroom with an inspiring resource or even (whisper it) *no lesson plan at all.* As you gain in experience, you will find that you need less and less detail in your plans. At this stage in your career, though, ensure that your plans have enough information to be reused at a later date.

fits the Curriculum

Ensure that you fit your plans to statutory requirements. You will have many wonderful and imaginative ideas for lessons, but remember to check whether they fit into the relevant statutory frameworks:

- In England visit
  www.education.gov.uk/schools/teachingandlearning/curriculum/primary
  www.education.gov.uk/schools/teachingandlearning/curriculum/secondary
- In Wales visit
  www.wales.gov.uk/topics/educationandskills/schoolshome/curriculuminwales and follow the link for either the Welsh or English version
- In Scotland visit www.educationscotland.gov.uk/thecurriculum
- In Northern Ireland visit www.nicurriculum.org.uk

Spend some time early on in the year talking through planning with your mentor. He or she will be able to advise you about how to plan, and also about what is required during your observed and formally assessed lessons. It's likely that you will have to plan in some detail for observed lessons, including information about special needs, differentiation, and so on.

Balanced lesson planning

Achieving a balance in your plans is vital for successful lessons, but it is tricky to achieve. With practice, you will find that you can instinctively sense what is balanced and what is not. However, this will only come by making mistakes and by being willing to experiment with different ideas and approaches. Balance essentially means that your lessons include a variety of strategies to help everyone learn effectively. By finding a good balance you will encourage your students to behave well. Here are some of my top tips for achieving a good balance in your lessons:

- *Put yourself in the children's shoes:* When planning, ask yourself how you would feel if you were presented with the activities you have in mind. There's a big difference between being asked to read a textbook in silence for an hour or being given 10 minutes' reading time with a mini whiteboard on which to make notes, before discussing what you have discovered with your group.

- *Make use of time limits:* Set a time limit for each task to ensure that the students stay focused and work to their maximum capacity. Time limits give a sense of forward momentum to a lesson and keep the children on task. Experiment with different time limits to see how your children respond; perhaps two or three minutes for a quick discussion activity or five to 10 minutes for something more complicated. Don't go beyond about 20 minutes without a change in task or direction, or a feedback session. While it's tempting to set your class to work so that you can step back, the optimum period for concentration is about this length of time.

- *Limit teacher talk:* The temptation to lecture and talk at your class is strong, but it's something that should, on the whole, be avoided. A good rule of thumb is not to talk to a primary class for more than the children's age plus two. Talk for much more than about 10 minutes to students of any age, and it's likely that they will drift off.

- *Maximise student activity:* Keep your students active to ensure that they stay involved in the lesson, and to discourage low level misbehaviour. Look for hands on, kinaesthetic style activities. Intersperse teacher talk with the chance for the students to do something (make notes, draw a mind map, doodle, get up and demonstrate, write on the board).

A balance of activities

There are many possible approaches to teaching and learning, and you can find some suggestions in the boxes below. The first box contains different types of teaching strategies. The second box suggests a variety of learning activities. Although some of the activities below are traditionally associated with particular subject areas, it is great fun to make unusual cross connections (a graph in English, a poem in science). Be experimental – students respond really well to the unexpected. In the third box you will also find a model balanced lesson plan which shows how you might put some of these approaches together.

You can also find lots more ideas in a downloadable list on my website www.suecowley.co.uk.

Teaching strategies

Teacher based:
- Teacher talks to the class
- Teacher gives instructions to the class
- Teacher discusses a topic, getting responses from the class
- Teacher asks questions of the students
- Teacher writes something on the board for the class to copy
- Teacher writes the students' ideas on the board for the class to work with

Student based:
- Students follow instructions
- Students work in pairs or groups
- Students make group presentations to the class
- Students make individual presentations to the class
- Students brainstorm in a group to get ideas
- Students work individually, e.g. reading, writing, drawing
- Students write their ideas on the board
- Students ask questions of the teacher
- Students make a list of questions they would like to research and answer

Types of learning activities

Reading activities:
- Individual reading
- Shared reading, e.g. whole class
- Reading for information/meaning
- Memorising facts, figures or vocabulary
- Reading in pairs or groups
- Speed or skim reading
- Reading newspaper or magazine articles
- Reading from textbooks
- Reading short cut out extracts
- Reading on a computer screen
- Reading each other's work
- Wordsearches and crosswords

Writing activities:
- Answering questions
- Summarising the main points of a text
- Note taking
- Writing reports
- Writing essays
- Imaginative writing – stories, poems
- Factual/analytical writing

Drawing activities:
- Drawing diagrams
- Drawing from life or photographs
- Drawing from imagination or memory
- Brainstorming
- Mind mapping

Speaking and listening activities:
- Discussions
- Explanations
- Drama exercises
- Role play and improvisations
- Question and answer sessions
- Quizzes
- Oral presentations
- Debates
- Making radio style programmes on a topic
- Listening to music

Physical and practical activities:
- Games and warm-ups
- Individual skills work
- Group exercises
- Drawing, modelling and painting
- Collage, sticking, sculpting
- Practical experiments
- Designing, building and testing
- Performances/demonstrations, e.g. dance, drama, science

A model balanced lesson plan

A balanced lesson plan of one hour might contain the strategies and activities given below. I have assumed an actual teaching time of 50 minutes, giving five minutes at the start of the lesson for the students to arrive/settle and five minutes at the end for clearing away. Although this lesson is for a writing-based subject, it could be adapted to fit a more practical area of the curriculum, for instance science or PE. This example is for a very straightforward lesson – once you've got the hang of balanced lessons you can play around with more experimental and practical approaches.

5 mins - Quick starter activity on the desks for when the students arrive
Student based, this helps to settle them ready for the lesson

5 mins - Teacher introduces the aim and topic of the lesson
Teacher talks, students listen

10 mins - Students brainstorm ideas on the topic in their books
Students find out for themselves what they already know

10 mins - Ideas are collated on the board and copied down
This brings everyone's ideas together

15 mins - Students do individual writing on the topic
Focus on individual written work for a limited time

5 mins - A couple of students read out their work
Brief oral presentation to the class for a plenary

Balance for the student

As well as balancing different strategies and activities, be aware of what you are asking the students to do during a lesson. Is there lots of emphasis on silent reading or writing, which requires a high level of concentration? Is there a great deal of noisy activity going on which may be disruptive for the quieter children (and other classes)? Again, put yourself in your students' shoes and think about how the lesson will actually feel for them.

Occasionally, your students will want to do very little during the lesson: be aware of when and why this might happen, and what you might do about it. There is little point in forcing your children to work in a particular way (e.g. writing in silence) if you are going to have to create confrontation in order to do so, and if the work they produce is unlikely to be of any value. For instance, a class that you see last lesson on a Friday, who have just had an hour of PE on a really hot day, are unlikely to be in the right mood to work particularly hard. Don't feel guilty about applying flexibility at times like this, and finding different approaches to try.

Balance for the teacher

While taking your students' needs into account, do not forget yourself. Ensure that there is a balance within the lesson for you – that you are not doing all the work or all the talking. When you first start teaching, your natural enthusiasm may encourage you to put huge amounts of energy into every lesson that you teach. As the school year drags on, and your energy starts to run out, you will see why it is so important to find balance for yourself within lessons. Here are some tips about how to do this:

- *Don't be too controlling:* As a new teacher it is tempting to over control your lessons, by using lots of teacher input (the 'chalk and talk' style). The temptation is to lead from the front because this makes you feel more secure in managing behaviour. This is a mistake though, as teacher-led lessons will often lead to behaviour problems because the students aren't *doing* all that much and they get bored. Hand over the reins to your children and see what happens. Yes, it might be chaotic and noisy at first, but often the best learning happens when the students are working in small groups or individually. Stand back and support/help out as required.

- *Give yourself some time out:* Aim for at least one period of quiet, calm individual work in most lessons, preferably with the children working in silence. This will give you a rest from the noise created by a class of students. It will also free you up to go around and help any individuals who need extra attention.

- *Take a lesson off:* From time to time, you may need a lesson off: don't feel bad about this. For some ideas about restful lessons have a look at 'Lessons for the tired teacher' in Chapter 4. Although the students may feel that they work really hard at school, it is the teacher who makes the majority of the effort in most classroom situations. Give yourself a break when you need it.

Short-term planning

Short-term planning is daily and weekly, and perhaps also half-termly, planning. These are the plans that you refer to for each lesson, which give you an outline of what you are going to teach. For some teachers these short-term plans will be very detailed, while for others they will only act as a brief reminder of what is to be covered. The tips below will help you when working on your own short-term planning:

- *Balance your week:* As well as balancing each individual lesson, try also to balance your week so that you don't have too many teacher-intensive sessions in one day or on consecutive days. You will get tired towards the end of the week, so aim to factor in some restful work at this stage, particularly on Friday afternoons.

- *Balance your marking:* When you are looking at your overall plans for the week, create a rota for marking, so that you cover each class or subject adequately, and so that you don't have huge amounts of marking all at one time. Identify specific pieces of work or topic areas (to yourself and to the students) that will receive more intensive marking. It can help to draw a brief overview of your week's lessons to see how your marking load falls.

- *Be flexible:* If a topic or lesson is going particularly well, or is taking longer than anticipated, it might be appropriate to spend more time on it than you had originally planned. Allow yourself this flexibility, so that you respond to the mood and the reactions of your children. Never feel that a plan is set in stone and cannot be adapted as necessary.

Long-term planning

Long-term planning means planning for an entire term or for the whole year. Your school or department may ask you to set out in advance what you intend to cover, but they will not expect you to stick rigidly to a long-term plan. Long-term planning offers a way of balancing resources within a department or school. For instance, if only one set of books is available for a particular topic, efficient long-term planning helps ensure that they are available at the appropriate time. Long-term planning also checks whether you have covered all areas of the curriculum. Most schools will have ready-made schemes of work for you to use or adapt. If these are not offered – do ask. Here are some tips for effective long-term planning:

- *Be flexible:* Just as with short-term planning, flexibility is crucial in your long-term plans. There are many variants, for instance a topic may take far less time than you had anticipated, or you may find that the students are particularly enjoying an area of a subject and you would like to spend more time on it.

- *Plan for variety:* Cover topics in a way that gives the students variety in their lessons. For instance, you could start by covering an area of your subject that necessitates a lot of individual work, and then follow this up with a group project. Similarly, a series of practical experiments or exercises could be followed by written review work.

- *Take an overview of the marking load:* Just as with short-term planning, take your marking load into consideration. You might plan to do some group discussion work just after a series of tests, or you could timetable in some practical activities at the end of a long written project. Avoid having a huge pile of marking right at the end of term – you don't want to spend your holidays doing it.

- *Know your syllabus:* If you are a secondary school teacher delivering a course at GCSE or AS/A level, you will have to cover all the areas in the syllabus. It is far better to finish early than to run out of time. If you have covered all the topics before the exams, you can devote the rest of the time to revision.

Planning shortcuts

During your training you will have been asked to give a large amount of detail in your planning and there are good reasons for this. When you first start teaching you are learning and experimenting and it is important for your tutors to see what you are doing and why. Although it may not have felt like it at the time, while you were training you had much more time to spend on planning lessons than you do now. Once you're in a 'real' teaching job, you have almost a full timetable and a large administrative workload.

Should you continue to plan in such detail? In short, no. Find lots of ways to keep time spent on planning to a minimum, because you need time for all the other parts of your role. Here are my top time saving tips and ideas:

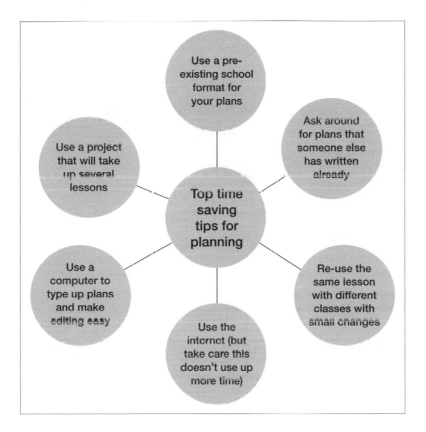

Use a pre-existing school format

If your school has a set format for lesson planning or schemes of work this will make life easier for you. The amount of detail you include can vary according to what suits your needs. Your school will also have created its format to fit with what inspectors are hoping to see, so this will keep you well on track for your assessed lessons.

Use ready-made plans

Don't reinvent the wheel! Teachers are notorious for redoing work which has already been done. If there are schemes of work and lesson plans already in existence, then use them as they are or with minor adaptations, scribbled onto a copy in note form. Ask other teachers in your school or department for advice on lessons that work well for them in each particular topic area, or with specific age groups.

Reuse your own material
If you are a secondary school teacher, delivering the same material to more than one class, use the same lessons with each one. Make some minor changes each time so that you don't become bored and stale in your lesson delivery.

Use the internet
These days there are literally thousands of ready-made ideas, plans, schemes of work and resources online. However, take care that this actually saves you time – searching online for the right plans can be a lengthy process.

Use a computer
If a basic outline format for planning is available, you will save a lot of time by filling this in on a computer. Many of the details will stay the same for a class from lesson to lesson (for instance any SEN information or details of children who need differentiated work).

Use a project
In the first edition of this book, written over 12 years ago, I wrote that projects are 'perhaps less fashionable than they used to be'. Funnily enough, since the original time of writing, cross curricular projects have come right back into fashion! (This just shows how approaches in teaching are cyclical – if you wait long enough they do come back into favour.) I have had great success using projects with my students. Projects are useful for a variety of reasons:

- They take up a number of lessons, which means less planning for you.
- The activities in a project are typically very engaging for the students.
- The tasks require independent learning and encourage the children to be self motivated.
- Less able students can access the work at an appropriate level.
- More able or keen children can do extension activities outside of lesson times.

- The plan for some project-based lessons can be brief and quick to prepare (for instance, a worksheet with a list of numbered tasks).

Planning engaging lessons

I feel very strongly that it is vital to engage children in what they are learning; to make them *want* to participate in lessons, rather than feeling that it is something that they are being forced to do. This is not to say that it is possible all the time – you must work out for yourself how much time and effort you are willing and able to put into this style of planning. But making your lessons engaging has many potential benefits:

- It makes the learning seem relevant and valuable.
- You should get good (or at least better) behaviour from your students.
- It shows the children that learning can be fun.
- Planning these lessons allows you to use your creative talents.
- It makes planning an imaginative and enjoyable experience.
- You can use engaging lessons as a reward for good work or behaviour.

At first, engaging lessons may feel risky and tricky to handle. However, as you teach them you will be learning really important lessons about how to manage your classroom and the behaviour of your students. If you're worried about how the class will react, get a few volunteers up to the front to handle those exciting resources, rather than letting everyone do the activity all at once.

It's tempting to believe that older students will not react as well as their younger counterparts to unusual or creative lessons. In my experience, though, I have found that they welcome them with open arms. Of course, not every lesson needs to be some kind of extravaganza of multi sensory wizardry. It's about balance – some days you will only have the energy for a 'the worksheets are on your desks' kind of lesson, other days you will feel like doing a really special or unusual session with your children. Certainly, you can usually add a simple resource to a lesson to spice up even the dullest of activities. For instance, having some real fruit to handle when doing a pictogram of the children's favourite fruits. Here are some general tips and hints for planning engaging lessons:

Use props or objects
Children find something captivating about seeing a prop or object in the classroom that would not normally be there. For instance, the teacher who uses a 'magic box' to inspire a lesson on story writing.

Go multi-sensory
Most of the time in lessons, students mainly use the senses of sight, hearing and touch. Find ways to incorporate the senses of taste and smell to give them a richer sensory experience. For instance, they might chop up ingredients to make a pizza as part of a division activity in maths.

Use fictional settings and scenarios
Making your classroom into somewhere different can be very engaging and inspiring for the children. I'm a drama teacher though, and you may well be wondering how fictional settings or scenarios could apply to other areas of the curriculum. To give a couple of examples, a teacher delivering a lesson on bridges and spans might use a scenario in which the children work as engineers to find suitable materials to build a bridge across a shark infested river. A teacher looking at the solar system might ask the class to play the role of astronauts, and set up a spaceship (using rows of chairs) which then flies out through the solar system and past the different planets, learning about each one as they pass.

Make it topical
Lessons that are up to date, and which deal with issues of current interest to your children, will engage their interest and gain better motivation and behaviour. You might use the format of a popular television programme to deliver a lesson, for instance *Deal or No Deal* or *Who Wants to be a Millionaire*. You could take a story from the news and use it within a lesson.

Make it weird
When a teacher does something really strange it catches the students' attention and makes them curious. One highly original lesson I've heard about is the one in which a science teacher urinates into a bottle, distils the

results and then drinks it. I'm not sure what Ofsted would make of that. While you might not feel the urge to do anything quite that outrageous, try to incorporate some weird and unusual ideas occasionally when planning and delivering your lessons.

The teacher's planner

Many schools give teachers a planner in which to keep all their bits and pieces. These offer a very useful way of keeping all your important information in one place. The planner is a small (A5 size) or large (A4 size) book similar to the teaching practice file you would have used during your training. The planner contains:

- a yearly calendar
- a page for each day's lesson planning
- space for registers
- a page to write out your timetable
- various other sections for notes, orders, etc.

Teachers use these planners in a variety of ways: some fill them out religiously in advance for each day, giving lots of detail about the lessons they will be teaching; others use them in a more haphazard style, filling them out after lessons, perhaps as a reminder of what has been covered. It is useful to keep as much information as you possibly can in the planner, so it is all in one place and you can carry it around easily. For instance, if you are a secondary teacher, rather than using a mark book you could keep all your registers, seating plans and marks for each class in the same section of the planner. That way, after taking the register you can leave the planner open to refer to students' names, check who owes homework and so on. You could also write detentions in on the daily planning page, where you can cross them off when they have been served.

The register/homework/detentions page might look a little bit like this:

Name	09.03.12	Homework	Mark /40	Detention	Served?
Alnwick, Sam	X	X	33		
Burns, Anna	O	O	O		
Coe, Theo	X	X	27		
Smith, Daniel	X	O	O	X	No – chase
Verrinder, Taj	X	X	39		

In the sample above, you can see that Anna Burns was absent from the lesson and so does not owe homework. However, Daniel Smith did not hand in his homework, earning himself a detention, which he has not yet served and which the teacher needs to chase up.

When you receive your planner, wait a bit before filling in registers, as there will often be changes to class lists at the beginning of term. Rather than writing information out, it is easier and quicker to photocopy it to size and stick it in. Similarly, glue your school calendar in on the appropriate pages rather than spending valuable time writing it out. You will, of course, experiment to find your own way of using a planner. Whatever works best for you is what is right.

PART II

You and Your Classroom

Chapter 3
Behaviour management

What is this chapter about?

Managing behaviour is the biggest concern for many new teachers, because if you can't get your children to behave, then you won't be able to teach them properly. Be aware that behaviour management is a worry for many experienced teachers as well, so you are definitely not alone. You will probably make lots of mistakes in handling student behaviour in your first year – I know I did. But every time you make a mistake, you will learn from it, and hopefully do things better next time around. At this point, you need to arm yourself with lots of practical strategies for managing behaviour so that you understand how to achieve a positive working atmosphere, and also so that you know what you might try if things go wrong.

Depending on the type of school where you teach, classroom control may present only minor challenges, or it may be the most vital part of your job. Even in the easiest of schools, where most students are keen to do what you ask, the importance of effective behaviour management should not be underestimated. This chapter offers you lots of practical advice for handling this aspect of your first year. Next September, when you've got a year's experience under your belt, things will seem an awful lot simpler. At all times, stay calm and retain a sense of perspective. It really is not the end of the world when your students misbehave, even though it will probably feel like it at the time.

'At a glance' guides to behaviour management

Let's start with a couple of quick guides to show you the basic strategies that you need to use to manage behaviour effectively. In this first guide you can see the main tenets of what I call 'positive behaviour management'.

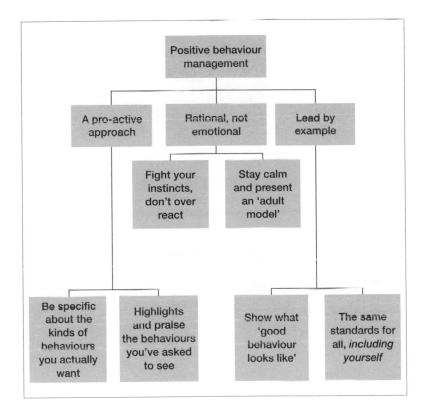

In this second guide, you can see how you might react to an incident of poor behaviour:

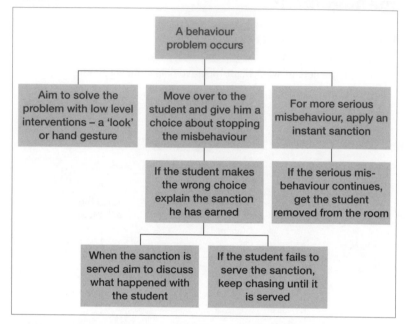

Understanding your school behaviour policy

Behaviour management is a complex skill, full of subtle techniques, many of which need to be learned 'on the job'. However, there is plenty you can do to arm yourself for the challenges ahead. Before you even set foot in the classroom, get yourself well prepared, by taking a long hard look at your whole school behaviour policy. This should be your 'behaviour bible' in your first year. Stick to the school policies and the students view you as a teacher who knows what is what. Be clear about the rules, and the options for sanctions and rewards, *before* you meet the students.

I was given a great tip in my own first year as a teacher. A deputy head teacher said to me 'blame the policy'. What he meant was, when you handle misbehaviour, make it clear that you are following the school systems. This helps depersonalise the situation, so you might say: *'Darren, I see that you have chosen not to work. In the school policy it says that students who refuse to work must serve a break-time detention. Please don't force me to punish you…'.*

Look in detail at your school policy and make sure that you can answer the following questions *before* your first lesson:

- What are the key school rules?
- What sanctions are available for me to use?
- Is there a graduated series of steps before I actually give a sanction?
- What sanctions does each type of misbehaviour 'earn'?
- What do I do if a student fails to serve a sanction?
- How do I pass on information about student behaviour to senior staff?
- What rewards are available for me to use?
- What is the procedure for contacting parents about behaviour (good or bad)?
- What paperwork do I need to fill out after an incident?
- In what circumstances can I send a student out of the room?
- What should I do in a crisis?

Types of misbehaviour

This year you will come across a whole host of different kinds of misbehaviour. Some are the typical childish behaviours that any parent knows well; others involve the serious and sometimes shocking issues that affect modern day schools. In the classroom it is sometimes the case that what starts as a fairly low level situation will escalate into a full blown incident. Learning how to avoid this is a key part of becoming an effective teacher.

Below is a list of some of the kinds of misbehaviour you might encounter. I have listed them in a rising scale of seriousness. As you are reading through the list, have a think about how you might react to and deal with each type of problem when it occurs in your classroom. Ask yourself the following questions:

- How will I feel if this happens?
- Will I be able to keep my cool?

- How am I likely to react?
- What is the best way to react?
- How serious do I consider this type of misbehaviour?
- Does this behaviour require an instant sanction?
- Do I know what my school policy says I should do?

Here are some of the misbehaviours that you might encounter:

- silliness
- forgetting equipment
- not doing homework
- chewing gum
- incorrect uniform
- calling out
- talking when the teacher is speaking
- 'blanking' the teacher
- cussing and name calling
- throwing paper/equipment
- swearing, but not *at* anyone
- chatting repeatedly
- refusal to complete work
- refusal to stay in a seat
- running around the room
- running out of the room
- complete refusal to comply with the teacher's requests
- fighting
- serious swearing (*at* you)
- throwing dangerous objects, e.g. chairs

Effective use of sanctions

Although sanctions are necessary for behaviour management, the ideal situation is to use them as little as possible. Let's be honest – no one likes to be punished, especially by a stranger. At the start, when the pupils don't know you very well, some of them may react in a very negative way to being sanctioned. That is not to say that you shouldn't punish them, just that when you do have to use sanctions you need to do it as effectively as possible.

Aim to use a rising scale of interventions – the list below gives you some ideas. Consider too, whether an intervention is required at all. You must use your professional judgement to decide whether calling attention to the misbehaviour is going to make the situation better or worse. As far as you can, stick to your school's behaviour policy to show that you are being fair and consistent. Some more serious misdemeanours will require an instant higher level response; the situations where this might happen will be outlined in your behaviour policy.

When a child misbehaves, you might try:

- The 'tactical ignore' (i.e. saying/doing nothing – this is particularly effective with attention seeking behaviour).
- Praising another child in the vicinity for good behaviour.
- Reminding the whole class about the rules.
- A pointed look.
- Moving towards the pupil.
- A click of the fingers in the child's direction.
- A hand on the child's desk to say *'I've spotted what's going on'*.
- A quiet word.
- A sharp word.
- A verbal warning.
- A written warning.
- A low level punishment (e.g. losing five minutes of break).
- Loss of a privilege such as golden time.
- A 'community' sanction such as picking up litter from the classroom floor.

- A same day detention.
- A longer or departmental detention.
- Letter or phone call home.
- Removal from the classroom by a senior member of staff.

Using the choice

The choice is a very useful technique for keeping calm when you have to apply sanctions. It will also help you avoid getting into confrontations with your students. The idea behind the choice is that it is up to the children to sort out their own behaviour. Your role is not about forcing them to do what you ask; instead you put the decision in their hands. Here's how it works:

Step one

- When a student misbehaves, make a statement about the behaviour you want.
- For instance, *'Jim, I want you to get on with your work now.'*

Step two

- If the student refuses to comply, offer a choice, outlining both the benefits of doing as you ask, and also the consequences of refusing.
- So, you might say: *'Jim, you have a choice. You can do the work now, and maybe even earn a merit. Unfortunately if you refuse to work now, I will have to keep you in at break to complete the task.'*
- Once you've outlined the choice, walk away, leaving the child to consider his or her options.

Step three

- Check after a minute or so to see if the student has made the right choice.
- If not, apply the sanction you outlined previously, making it clear that the student has 'chosen' this sanction by his misbehaviour.
- So, you could say: *'Jim, unfortunately I notice that you are still refusing to work. And that means that I have no option but to keep you in at break to complete it.'*

At this point, if the student starts to complain or tries to reason/negotiate with you, ignore what he says and move calmly away.

Making detentions work

Many secondary schools use detentions as the main form of sanction. They are also used fairly regularly at the upper end of the primary school. When you do have to give a detention, make sure that you do this in the best possible way. Here are some useful tips for getting the best out of detentions:

- Whenever possible, short detentions should take place with you supervising and on the same day as the misdemeanour occurs (i.e. during a break or for a very short time after school).

- It is absolutely *vital* that you remember to enforce detentions. If you don't turn up, or if the child fails to attend, the sanction is worthless.

- You might write the student's name down in your planner and then cross it off when the detention has been served.

- Consider what you and the child are going to do in the detention. Sometimes a punishment is appropriate, other times it is more effective to have a chat with the child about the behaviour and why it happened.

- Aim to make the punishment fit the crime – wiping tables as a sanction for grafitti, picking up litter as a sanction for dropping it, writing a letter of apology if inappropriate language has been used.

Dealing with the serious incident

Serious incidents are, thankfully, reasonably rare in most schools. When they do happen, the new teacher can be left feeling vulnerable and upset. Don't let the fear of abusive behaviour prey on your mind, but do be aware ahead of time what you should do if a serious incident occurs. Consider the following points:

- Know what your school policy says about dealing with a child who is out of control. If there is a 'red card' or 'panic button' option, be aware of exactly how it works. Often, it will involve sending a trusted child to get help from a senior member of staff who is 'on call', i.e. available in case of emergencies.

- Remember that the safety of the whole class is your responsibility. Remove other children from the immediate area, either by moving them to the side of the room, or lining them up outside.

- When handling a confrontational child, stay calm, keep your voice low and quiet, and make plenty of use of the child's name.

- Know what the guidelines are for dealing with violence and for restraining children (see below).

- After the event, take some time out to recover. If possible, sit with a friend in the staffroom and talk about what happened.

- Make sure that information about the situation gets passed on to senior staff. Write down an account of the serious incident while it is still fresh in your mind.

- Talk over what happened with an experienced member of staff, preferably your mentor. Does he or she have any advice or words of wisdom?

- Don't blame yourself or take it personally. Serious incidents are about the child and his or her personal situation, rather than about you as a teacher.

The government has recently clarified their advice to teachers on the use of reasonable force. For more information visit: www.education.gov.uk/aboutdfe/advice/f0077153/use-of-reasonable-force-advice-for-school-leaders-staff-and-governing-bodies/who-can-use-reasonable-force

Effective use of rewards

Rewards will always be more effective than sanctions in encouraging good behaviour. Children of all ages respond well to motivators, but the kind of reward that is useful and appropriate will depend a great deal on the age and outlook of the student. For some children, the only reward required is a sense of achievement, and the feeling that they are pleasing their teacher. The students who respond well to such intrinsic motivators are typically those from a background where learning is valued and supported. Other children need far more input, and far more obvious or extrinsic types of rewards.

These students may well be from a background where there is less positive reinforcement, and less support for learning from the home.

Although your behaviour policy should outline the school rewards system, there is often plenty of scope for the teacher's personal input and individual ideas. After all, you know what best suits the children in your class. On my website, you will find a long list of ideas for rewards, which I've gathered from schools around the UK (visit www.suecowley.co.uk/free-downloads.html). Some of the simplest rewards, which are in use in most schools, include:

- verbal praise
- a smile
- a sticker
- a stamp
- a certificate
- a star chart
- merits
- a praise assembly
- sweets
- golden time.

The first lesson

In your first lesson (or your first day in the primary school) concentrate on stamping your personality and expectations on your class. This is the time to create a climate for good behaviour. But how exactly do you do this? With experience, every teacher finds his or her own way, but here are some ideas about behaviour management for you to consider before your own first lesson:

- *Don't try to do too much:* Curriculum wise, don't plan anything too ambitious for your first lesson. You will probably spend much of the time on administrative tasks such as checking names on the register, sorting out seating plans, explaining where equipment is kept, giving out books and talking to the children about your expectations.

- *Have a confident persona:* The irony about getting good behaviour is that if you come across as nervous, your children will pick up on your uncertainty and respond by misbehaving. But of course it is only natural for an NQT to feel nervous in his or her first lesson. Try to hide your inner feelings and project a confident persona. At the very least, stay relaxed and try not to panic. It will help a great deal with your confidence levels if you have a clear understanding of how the whole school behaviour policy works.

- *Explain your rules clearly:* The temptation to dive straight into your first 'real' lesson may be overwhelming, but do spend some time (perhaps 10 to 15 minutes) discussing your ideas about classroom behaviour with your children. That way they know that you mean business and that you have a clear idea of your expectations. These rules give the children the set of boundaries that they need. This idea is covered in much more detail in the next section and in the model lesson in Chapter 4.

Creating a seating plan

The first lesson is the ideal time to introduce a seating plan, particularly with students in key stages 2 and 3. There are lots of good reasons why this is useful:

- It shows you are a teacher who is in control of his or her classroom.

- It's a great way to learn names.

- It stops students sitting in social groups, which can lead to lots of chat.

- You can always move away from a seating plan, but introducing one *after* your first lesson may be tricky.

Sometimes a seating plan is not such a good idea. For instance, with disaffected key stage 4 students, in a 'difficult' school, confrontations might arise. If you're unsure, check with other more experienced staff on the training day.

You may feel a bit nervous about arranging a seating plan. However, although it means spending time on organisation at the start of the lesson, it is time well spent. On the next page are some tips to help you get it right:

- Draw your plan ahead of time – if there are copies of the seating plan on the door, the walls and your desk, this makes it tricky for students to claim they 'don't know where to sit'.

- Seat the students in alphabetical order – you don't know them yet, so this makes sense and is the fairest way to do it. You can use 'learning names' as your excuse if you feel nervous about their reaction.

- If there is space, line the class up outside the room first – this allows you to make the entry to the classroom as smooth and uncomplicated as possible.

- Set a target – give the class a clear focus for getting to the right seats in a quick and sensible way.

- Offer a reward if they meet your target of sitting quickly and without a fuss, for instance a couple of minutes 'golden time' at the end of the lesson to relax.

- Use the register as a check – as you take the register for the first time, ensure that the children are seated as you had asked.

- Use 'free choice of seating' as a reward – offer this in the first lesson, but wait a while before you allow your class to move around. Make them earn it.

Setting the boundaries

Your tutors at college probably told you about the 'honeymoon period', the time when the students will do what you ask, before they have sussed you out. In most schools (although certainly not all) the students will sit and listen to you for the first couple of lessons, apparently absorbing every word you are saying. Then, just when you think it is safe to relax, they turn into the class from hell.

So, how can you avoid this situation? More experienced teachers may tell you that in a few years' time you will find it easy to control your children. This, however, is not much consolation when you are an NQT. The last thing you want is to spend a whole year suffering before you get a chance to make a fresh start with a new set of students. And believe me once you have 'lost' a class, it is extremely difficult to get them back. I say this from bitter experience of a class that I 'lost' in my own NQT year.

What the students need at the start of your time together is for you to set the boundaries for them. If you do this effectively, and *stick to it,* you will make life much simpler and easier for yourself and for them. If you fail to set the boundaries, then like children the world over, your students will push and push until they find out exactly how much they can get away with. When you first start out, it is tricky to do, because it's hard to know exactly what you can and should expect. Plus, you won't want to come across as mean or unreasonable.

A teacher in an FE college told me a brilliant story about how he explains his boundaries. In his first lesson with a class, he draws a line on the board and asks the students what it is. When they say *'a line'*, he tells them *'that's right – now just make sure you don't step over it'*. When you set boundaries this is what you are doing – drawing a line in the sand and saying 'you can do anything on this side of the line, but the stuff on the other side is forbidden'. The younger your students, the clearer you will need to be about exactly what is and is not alright. Your message to the children is: *This is how we do things here.*

To set the boundaries effectively, you need to:

- Think carefully ahead of time about what is and is not okay in your classroom.

- Use the school behaviour policy and school rules as a basis for your boundaries.

- Spend time talking about your boundaries at the start of your first lesson.

- Keep your boundaries clear and simple – start with no more than three main rules.

- Use positive statements of the behaviour you want, rather than negative ones about what you don't.

- Use the word 'we' for your statements to suggest a sense of inclusivity – the teacher must do these things as well as the students.

- Talk with your children about the reasons for having these boundaries, the rewards they can expect if they follow them, and the sanctions they will get if they don't.

- Some teachers like to get the students to set their own rules or boundaries, to build a feeling of teamwork.

- Make a list of rules to go on your classroom wall – this should be big and clear.

- Refer to your list regularly, for positive behaviour as well as negative.

- Talk again about your boundaries at the end of the lesson, the start of the next – again and again until the students understand that you are not planning to give in on these key expectations.

Although most schools have similar expectations of student behaviour, the way that these are expressed varies quite a bit. You can find some suggested rules below to give you a starting point for setting your own boundaries. For each of the rules I've given a brief description of how you might introduce this rule to your class – how it works and why it is important. Remember that you need to adapt and rephrase these rules to suit your own age group.

Rule: We listen in silence when someone is talking
This applies to teacher, support staff and students. It's polite, respectful and it means we can get on with the lesson. You might also express this as: *One person speaks at a time.*

Rule: We arrive at lessons ready and prepared to learn
This means you arrive on time, with your equipment/kit, with a positive attitude about the learning. That way we can get on with our lessons and enjoy ourselves.

Rule: We show respect to each other at all times
This includes no swearing, no shouting, no aggression, etc. I will respect you and I expect you to do the same.

Rule: We work to the best of our ability
Be willing to try hard and to push yourselves, and make sure you do homework. I will put lots of effort into preparing interesting lessons and supporting you.

Ten tried and tested teaching tips

New teachers are constantly bombarded with information and advice, and it can all seem a bit overwhelming at times. This is particularly true with behaviour management, because it is a complex and subtle skill for you to acquire, and there are many different approaches that might work in any given situation. I would like to offer you ten practical and straightforward tips to refer to early on in the year or at moments of crisis or despair when it all seems to be going wrong. The tips in the following ten boxes are a useful summary of the things that I learned during my NQT year.

---

1. Perfect the deadly stare

As a teacher, you have access to many different forms of communication, both verbal and non-verbal. Perhaps the most effective way of communicating your feelings is the 'deadly stare'. Perfect this and you may never have to ask for silence again. You will be able to walk into a classroom and silence your students with a glance. There is no easy way of describing the deadly stare, but you will know when you have perfected it. The deadly stare says: *'I am the teacher, I am in charge, and if you do not close your mouth, stop talking and wait for my commands, you are likely to suffer in the most horrible way known to humankind. So, be sensible, be quiet and let's get on with the lesson.'* And all that without opening your mouth! The deadly stare might include all or some of the following elements:

- A quick fixed stare at an individual who is not doing what you wish.
- A raised eyebrow to show your surprise at a student's temerity.
- A pursed mouth to show disapproval.
- A furrowed brow.

Your stare won't always need to be 'deadly' – you might also want to go for 'disappointed' or 'sad' or simply 'I'm waiting'. With younger children adapt the 'deadliness' of your stare so that you don't frighten them.

---

2. Wait for them

If there was only one piece of advice I could give teachers about behaviour management, it would be this: *wait for them*. If you follow this strategy from the start, your children will know that it is the way you work. Do not open your mouth to teach until you have *complete* silence, and I mean complete. Do not start talking until every single student is looking directly at you. Even if you have to use a million different strategies to gain their attention, eventually they should come to you. And even if they won't come to you, don't give in and talk over them, try a different teaching method instead (for instance, writing instructions on the board). If you talk over your class at the start, it will only get worse.

This idea is so useful and important that I am going to repeat it again. *Do not open your mouth until you have complete and total silence and every student is sitting still and looking at you.* Fold your arms, look impatient, check your watch, take out the novel you are in the middle of reading, do some knitting, gaze at the view out of the window, but on no account talk to a class of students who are not listening.

There are a number of reasons why doing this is so crucial:

- First and foremost, it means good quality teaching and learning can take place.
- It stamps a considerable amount of authority on you for very little effort.
- If you do choose to talk over the students, you are effectively saying 'go ahead and talk, I don't mind'.
- You are also saying, to the child who is talking, 'it's okay for you to talk, it's just not okay for any of the others'.
- At first, a few children may chat quietly, but after a while everyone else will join in.

It can seem scary at first, but if you wait the vast majority of classes will come to you, especially in your very first lesson. If you start to panic and feel you must intervene, you might try:

- Using tips 1 and 10 – the deadly stare and praise one, encourage all.

- A non-verbal signal, such as three claps.
- Moving to stand beside a student who is still talking.
- Moving over to a group who *are* listening and chatting quietly to them while you wait for the rest of the class to fall silent.
- Writing 'whole class detention?' and a circle on the board and adding minutes to this.

In some very difficult schools, these low level strategies may not work, and you might have to resort to more unusual or extreme approaches. The key is to keep trying until you find something that works – be the teacher who refuses to give up. (In one particularly tricky school, it took me almost a term with one class, but I got there eventually.) For some examples of other useful strategies, see my book *Getting the Buggers to Behave*.

3. Always set a time limit

Your children *want* boundaries: they are still unsure of where they stand in the world and what is expected of them. Even as adults we crave the security of knowing what we are expected to do. So, when you set a task make sure your students know how long they have to complete it – whether it is three minutes, 20 minutes or five lessons. Think about how people work – we are always more efficient when we have a deadline to meet – and use this to your advantage in the classroom.

Once you have set your time limit and allowed the students to start working on the task, give them a constant reminder of how long they have left. Your actual measuring of the time can be flexible according to how quickly you think the students are progressing (two minutes can always be stretched to three). Alternatively, you could say to them, *'When you see that it's 10 past 10, I'd like you all to stop working and wait for the next instruction. I'm not going to remind you about the time, I'd like to see how well you can observe this time limit yourselves.'* When the deadline arrives, some of the more observant students will notice and stop working. As the noise levels drop, the others will join in until everyone falls silent.

4. Strike a balance

Teaching is about balance in so many ways, but this is one of the hardest things to achieve. You need to develop a sense of 'where the students are coming from', as a teacher in my first school used to say. By this I mean you should learn to:

- Adapt your teaching style to suit the class and the children.
- Change lesson content/format/delivery to suit the class.
- Use a verbal approach that sits well with the students.
- Apply sanctions and rewards in a way that suits them.

As you gain in experience, you will use a very different attitude and style with a class of 15-year-olds and with one of 11-year-olds, or with the well-motivated five-year-olds in your class, and their less enthusiastic peers. Make sure that what you ask for, and how you phrase it, matches the class and the children. Here are some tips about learning to strike a balance:

Be willing to negotiate: Although most of the time you should give an aura of complete certainty, learn when negotiation and flexibility might be appropriate. For instance, a bottom set in an examination year may be completely disillusioned with school. If they feel they are not going to do well in their exams, they will resent a teacher who tries to force them to work hard all the time. Far better to be realistic: if they work solidly for 20 minutes, they could earn a five minute break for a chat.

Respond to the 'mood' of the class: Your class will often arrive in a 'mood' – good, bad, tired, grumpy, indifferent. This can be influenced by the weather, the time of the week, or some other external factor. In the secondary school, perhaps their previous lesson went badly; in the primary school, maybe there was a confrontation at lunchtime. If you sense that your class is full of enthusiasm and in the mood for hard graft, capitalise on this by getting through lots of work. If you feel that the class is overexcited, spend some time calming your children down. If your class seems down and in a foul mood, work hard to create a positive atmosphere.

Show that you're human: While you need to start out firm with your children, and stick with a fairly strict approach, there will be moments when you can hint at the fact that you are a human being. This might mean laughing at yourself when you make a stupid mistake; it could mean giving your class a 10 minute break at the end of a particularly long hard day.

5. Quiet teachers get quiet classes

When I was a trainee teacher, on one teaching practice I worked with a class that had two teachers, one for Monday to Wednesday and one for Thursday and Friday. One teacher spoke really quietly to the class and the other was much louder. The difference in the classroom noise levels amazed me. With the quiet teacher, the children had to listen really carefully, and the class was quieter as a whole. With the loud teacher, they were almost like a different set of children – much more excitable, much harder to settle. A big advantage of being a quiet teacher is the saving you will make on your voice. For many NQTs, a strained voice is a real problem, leading to sore throats and time off work. A quiet class is also generally less stressful and your children will be calmer and easier to handle. Here are some tips for becoming a quiet teacher:

Learn to hear yourself: Take a moment when you are teaching to listen to yourself. How loud are you? And just how loud do you really need to be? Consider the tone of your voice as well, and whether you sound strained or relaxed. This will transmit itself to the children, and have a direct effect on their work and behaviour.

Learn to turn the sound down: As you listen to yourself, imagine you are turning the volume down on a stereo and aim to do the same with your voice. Very often, we speak much more loudly than is actually necessary.

Try not to talk too much: When you first start teaching, it is very tempting to do a lot of talking at your class. You might feel more in control when you are teaching from the front, but this puts a strain on your voice and is often ineffective as a teaching strategy. If you talk for a long time, it is likely that you will raise the volume gradually, without even realising it. Keep teacher talk to a minimum, and student participation to a maximum.

6. Avoid confrontation (a.k.a. 'you get what you give')

Teaching can be a stressful and frustrating job. Unless you are a naturally super calm person, there will most likely be days in your first year when you lose your cool, raise your voice, or shout at the class. But the problem is, if you become confrontational with the children, they may respond aggressively in return, or at the very least they will find it amusing to watch you lose your temper. Your aim must be to stay as calm as you possibly can, and to model a controlled, adult approach to every situation.

Confrontations can arise for many reasons. You're human, and sometimes controlling 30 or more students is exhausting. Sometimes a child will treat you in a totally unacceptable way, and the natural response is to give as good as you get. One of your key aims this year must be to learn to ignore or defuse your instinctive, emotional response. Here are some useful tips about staying calm and avoiding confrontation:

Take a breath: It sounds obvious, doesn't it? But you'd be amazed at how easy it is to literally stop breathing in the classroom. Before you deal with *any* misbehaviour (except where two students are literally about to kill each other, or do something extremely serious), pause and take a few deep breaths. It's very rare to find a situation where an instant response is required – far better to calm yourself down before you attend to your children.

Build a barrier: The normal human reaction to an aggressive encounter is to become angry or upset. Many teachers are faced by confrontational behaviour on a regular basis, so we need to find ways of taking a reasoned and professional approach. Build a metaphorical barrier between you and the confrontational child, so that any poor or abusive behaviour simply 'bounces off' your defences. That is not to say don't deal with the misbehaviour, but aim not to let it get to you.

Don't take it personally: It is very tempting to feel that an abusive student is picking on you personally, and to give an emotional response to the 'attack'. In fact the child is often simply responding to a situation that he or she finds hard to deal with (perhaps being told off, or being asked to work on a task she finds tricky). Try to view the behaviour as separate from the child, and see it as a symptom of a deeper problem, rather than any personal reflection on you as a person or as a teacher.

Choose sympathy over anger: Any child who becomes confrontational with a teacher clearly has a problem of some sort. View the aggressive individual with sympathy rather than anger. This approach also helps to take the wind out of the aggressive child's sails and to make it less likely that things will escalate.

Apply reason to the situation: Using your calm and unruffled persona, talk to the child about what is going on. Encourage the student to discuss his or her behaviour and what has caused it. Talk to the child about what will happen if the behaviour continues, for instance that you will have no option but to apply a sanction.

7. Give one instruction at a time

As we will see in tip 8 ('Explain, repeat, explain'), it is surprisingly difficult to give clear instructions. It is tempting to give your class a long list of instructions to follow, particularly if you are setting a complicated task. Remember though that is is hard for children to take in and retain a lot of information at once. It works far better to give one instruction at a time, stopping between each one to ensure that the students have understood what you want them to do. Again, this will avoid problems with misunderstandings and students continually asking what they have to do.

As an alternative, consider breaking longer sets of instructions down into their individual components, and getting the students to complete each component at a time. For instance, if the activity requires lots of resources, you might first give the instructions for each group to collect what they need and place them in the middle of their tables.

When you are giving instructions, you may find that the children are so eager to get started on the activity that they go to start work the minute you pause for breath. A very useful way of avoiding this is to state at the beginning: *'When I say "go" I want you to...'*. If your children jump up, ready to get started, stop them by asking *'Did you hear me say "go" yet?'* They will quickly be trained to wait for you to finish, and to say *'Ready, steady, go!'*

8. Explain, repeat, explain

One of the biggest problems the inexperienced teacher faces is the frustrations caused by misunderstandings in the classroom. You know the scenario from teaching practice: you spend five minutes explaining to the class what you want them to do, you set them off to work, then a few seconds later three hands go up 'Miss/Sir, I don't understand... what did you say I have to do?' It is actually surprisingly difficult to give clear and straightforward instructions that your children will understand. This is one of many key skills that you have to acquire during your first few years in the job.

Remember that the children are being bombarded with new information, particularly at the start of term and especially those new to a school. Young children may have a limited vocabulary and find it hard to retain lots of information at once. Similarly, children who do not have English as their first language may also find it hard to assimilate instructions. So, use the 'explain, repeat, explain' strategy:

1. *Explain:* Tell the class what you want them to do, preferably giving a visual example at the same time. Keep your explanation as concise as you can.

2. *Repeat:* Ask a student to repeat what you just said (you might choose someone who looks as if they weren't listening). If this student is not able to explain the task, ask for someone who can to raise a hand. By hearing the students' interpretation, you may also find out that they did not actually understand your instructions properly.

3. *Explain:* Repeat the instructions again in your own words, clarifying any areas of uncertainty, and then ask: *'Is there anyone who's not sure what we're going to do?'*

This might sound a bit patronising, but it really does help clarify any misunderstandings and also encourages the children to listen carefully the first time. There may be genuine misunderstandings taking place, perhaps because you are not experienced in giving clear instructions, or the students are not yet used to your way of working.

9. Put yourself in their shoes

This tip is worth following whenever something or someone is frustrating you. That brilliant lesson you spent three hours planning is going wrong? Put yourself in your children's shoes and try to see it from their point of view. What would they say is wrong with it? Why exactly are they looking so bored? (You might even be brave enough to ask them.) The students at the back of the class keep talking and passing love notes while you are trying to explain the finer points of quadratic equations. Put yourself in their shoes – you were young once, sometimes school can be just plain boring, no matter how good the teacher is. Develop high levels of empathy, and constantly remind yourself what it was like to be a kid. This will help you evaluate the work you set, and the way you teach, from a far more objective viewpoint.

10. Praise one, encourage all

You were probably told at university that praise is a very effective teaching tool. However, generalised praise, although useful, has its limitations. Next time you want a class to behave in a certain way, try singling out one individual who is already doing what you want. *'That's great, Sundip, it looks like you're ready to get on with the lesson, because you're sitting really quietly and waiting for me to take the register. Thank you.'* This is far more effective than moaning at the class to be quiet. It is also a useful backup tip for getting silence – do give it a try, you may be pleasantly surprised at how quickly and easily it works.

Learning names

Learning your children's names is absolutely vital for good behaviour management; it's all part of building a good and strong relationship with them. However, there is no overestimating how difficult learning names can he. This is particularly true for secondary school teachers of subjects such as PE, music, drama and RE, who may have a large number of classes which they see for only an hour a week each.

Until you have a good idea of the children's names, it is very hard to control them effectively. A reprimand is always much more powerful if you can use the student's name; similarly, praise is far better if you can personalise it. You will probably find it fairly easy to learn the names of the 'good' children, who always answer questions, and the 'naughty' ones, who are always messing around. However, when it comes to writing reports, it can be extremely embarrassing if you cannot remember which student fits which name (or even which gender they are). Here are a few ideas that have worked for me:

- Use an alphabetical seating plan, and refer to it as you take the register.

- In the first few lessons, use sticky name labels or get the children to make name plates to put on their desks.

- Use the children's names as often as possible, whenever you address them.

- Make a few subtle annotations on your register (nothing rude, just in case a child or an inspector looks at it!).

- Try out some memory systems to improve your memory – Tony Buzan's books are a great starting point.

Another useful approach is to play name games with your class, particularly in the first few lessons. These are fun and useful for reinforcing names (both for you and for your students). Here are a few suggestions:

- *The adjective game:* The students find an adjective to describe themselves, starting with the same letter as their name, e.g. 'My name is Sue and I am stupendous.'

- *Pass the name:* To start, the student says their own name, and then the name of the person they are passing to. Anyone who pauses or makes a mistake is out. 'Tim to Anna, Anna to Chirag, Chirag to Shami', and so on. Ask the students to pass to someone of the opposite sex, to make it harder and to avoid friends passing to friends all the time.

- *Pass the name (version two):* This is a combination of the two games above and requires the students to remember each other's adjectives: 'Terrible Tim to Anxious Anna, Anxious Anna to Careful Chirag, Careful Chirag to Silly Shami', and so on.

The delicate art of bluff

For the secondary school teacher with a large number of students (perhaps seen only once a fortnight), sometimes it proves nigh on impossible to remember all the names. The week of reports comes and you are panicking. You only have one more lesson with these students before you have to comment on them. What can you do? Here are a few strategies you could try, involving the 'gentle art of bluff':

- *Question and answer:* Ask a question using the name of a specific student and then look to see who answers.

- *State your name:* Set a group or individual task and ask the students to state their names before they start their presentation.

- *Off you go:* Ask the children to stand behind their chairs or get ready to leave in name order. When you call out the names of the children you do not know, look to see who moves.

- *Ask for help:* Ask a child you can trust to be discreet for the name that you cannot remember. They will be delighted that you have asked for their assistance.

- *Name your reward:* Give out merit marks (or whatever rewards your school uses) and as you write them into the student's diary, check the name on the front.

Your teaching style

As you look around your school and overhear students talking about other members of staff, you will begin to see how teachers each have their own individual teaching style. This is especially so when it comes to managing behaviour. The style you use is entirely a matter of personal taste: it depends on your personality and also on the kind of students you are teaching. My experience suggests that some approaches are far more effective than others. Consider the impact of the following aspects of your own teaching style.

What you wear

The way you dress will vary according to the age range you teach, your subject specialism and the type of school you work in. For instance, if you are a PE or drama teacher, you may need to wear loose clothing so that you can demonstrate activities for the students. If your school has a strict uniform code for the children, it is likely that the head expects the staff to dress smartly as well. As a new teacher, avoid wearing casual clothing. If you dress smartly you give your children the impression that you mean business. Your class will be making judgements about you from the moment they meet you, and the way that you dress is part of this.

What you say

The phrases you use and the way you speak will communicate your style to the children. This will be both about the way that you set work, and also about how you maintain order. You should talk to your students in a very different way to that in which you talk to your friends in a social situation. If you are a secondary teacher, your speaking style will also vary according to the age of the class you're working with. We all adapt the way we speak according to the situations we are in and the impression we want to give, so be aware of this, particularly in your early lessons. Aim for a speaking style that is:

- clear-cut
- straightforward
- relaxed
- interesting

- engaging
- consistent
- controlled.

How you maintain order

The way you create discipline (or fail to) will give out strong messages about your teaching style. The ideal situation is for the students to view you as firm but fair, and hopefully a little bit fun as well. You should apply exactly the same rules for every child, but be aware that certain situations and individuals will call for careful handling. Aim to keep order in a way that is:

- calm
- confident
- assertive
- assured
- certain
- aware

- positive
- firm
- consistent
- structured
- flexible where appropriate.

How you set and mark work

The way in which you set work, and mark the results, will affect the way your students perceive you and the way they behave for you. If your lessons are interesting, well structured and have clear aims, you will maintain your children's interest and keep them engaged in their learning. If you set lots of work that you ask the students to complete quickly, but fail to mark, they will view you as unreasonable. On the other hand, if you never set homework and allow the children to work at their own pace, they may well like you, but whether they will respect you is another matter. The teacher's expectations about the work that will be done play a vital role in communicating his or her style, and in setting up a climate for good or bad behaviour.

What you do

Teachers should avoid saying one thing and doing another. If you expect your children to behave well, but you treat them without respect, you are storing up trouble for yourself. If you set the boundaries at the start and stick to them in a fair manner, the children will know where they stand. This might not happen instantly, but stick at it and things will improve. It is important for you to have interests outside school. Your students want to feel that you are a person as well as a teacher. Take an interest in wider issues, including the latest cultural and technological developments. Aim to comment on matters that are of interest to your students, and incorporate them into your lessons where possible.

How you set up your classroom

If you are a primary teacher, or a lucky secondary teacher, you will have a space of your own, a classroom that you teach in all the time. The students will make judgements about you by looking at your room, and consequently make decisions about how they are going to behave, often at a subconscious level. This process will be taking place right from the very first moment they arrive at your class. There are a number of ways in which you can influence behaviour through the way you set up your room:

- *Personalise the space:* Before the first lesson of the year, spend some time personalising your classroom space. This helps stamp your mark on the room and shows that you are in control. Put a sign on the door with your name and class/subject. Pin up a set of rules, rewards and sanctions to show that you know what the policy says. Perhaps create some displays about the work that you'll be doing at the beginning of term, or put up some colourful posters.

- *The layout of the room:* There is a temptation to maintain the status quo in the way that your room is laid out, particularly when you are new to a school. However, there is no reason at all why you should not change the layout of your room to suit your own teaching needs and style. Perhaps you might want to turn the desks to face in a different direction, or create different learning zones in the primary classroom. Again, this will help show the children that this is your space, one in which you maintain overall control.

- *The layout of the desks:* Setting out a classroom in rows gives a very different message to grouping the tables. Similarly, a U-shape arrangement will send a very different signal. This is a matter of personal opinion as well as being dictated by the type of room you have. See the following section for more on this.

Managing the space

Think carefully about how practical your classroom layout is before the year begins. At the lower end of the primary range, there can be quite a lot of flexibility about how different areas of your room are arranged. You might have a place for art, another for sand and water work, a carpet for stories and whole class discussions, and some desks for written activities. If you do plan to make a lot of changes to a lower primary classroom, it is worth drawing some plans before you start reorganising the furniture.

Higher up the primary school, and in the secondary school, desks are often arranged either in rows or in groups. There is no reason why you should not start with the desks in rows and then change the layout later in the term. There is also no reason why you should not move furniture for specific lessons, but there are administrative problems associated with this that you must deal with. If you are a secondary school teacher using someone else's classroom, you will make yourself extremely unpopular if you move the furniture, but do not return it to its previous position.

The plus and minus sides of three of the most popular classroom layouts are explained below:

Desks in rows

✓ *Advantages:* All the students face the front, which makes it easier to check that they are listening and allows everyone to see the board easily. You can give out and collect in resources and books along each row. The students will view you as a 'traditional' style teacher, which can be useful with a class where behaviour is difficult.

✗ *Disadvantages:* It is hard to do any meaningful group or discussion work without substantially rearranging the furniture. There is the temptation to ignore the ends of rows, because you cannot see the students so easily. You will only be able to give help to two students at a time. This style of layout tends to encourage 'chalk and talk' style teaching, i.e. the teacher stands at the front, talking to the class and writing notes on the board.

Desks in groups

✓ *Advantages:* Group work and discussions can take place easily, and you can talk to a whole group of students at one time. You are generally encouraged to move around the classroom more; as a result this layout encourages an interactive style of teaching.

✗ *Disadvantages:* The students may not be able to see the board so easily. It is harder to ensure that all students are paying attention if some of them have their backs to you. It can be harder to give out resources. In a poorly-behaved class, the children could interpret this layout as the sign of a relaxed teaching style.

Desks in a U-shape

✓ *Advantages:* This is an excellent layout for whole class discussions and debates. It is straightforward to hand out resources and all the students are able to see the board.

✗ *Disadvantages:* This layout can make group work tricky. It can be difficult to fit desks into this arrangement if you have a lot of students, or teach in a very cramped classroom.

Creating groups

For many activities you will need the students to work in groups, and creating these is a challenge in itself. I would advise against planning group work when you are very new to your class or classes. Spend a little time on individual or pair work first, so that when you first attempt a group activity the students have a very clear idea about your expectations of their behaviour. Before starting on group work, consider the following points:

- *Moving the furniture:* If your desks are laid out in rows, allow sufficient time for moving the furniture and returning it to its former position. Rather than having a free-for-all, take time over this and ask one group of students at a time to rearrange their desks. Decide beforehand on the best layout of desks for the type of work you want to do and draw this up on the board for the students to follow.

- *Combinations:* Keep a careful eye on the combinations in each group. Ensure that any troublemakers are kept separate, as they have a tendency to gravitate to each other. Ensure too that there is a good mix in each group, with leaders as well as followers. Be wary about putting too many strong personalities together.

- *Teacher vs student groupings:* Before you start on some group work, decide whether you are going to create the groups yourself, or whether you will allow the students to do this. If you are only doing the occasional bit of group work, there is probably no harm in allowing the children to decide on groupings for themselves. However, if group work plays an essential part in your subject or

at your age level, you need to set the groups yourself to ensure that
the children work with a variety of people, rather than just with
their friends. You will also probably want to group by ability level
for some subjects. Teacher-chosen groupings avoid the situation
where one child is left out.

- *A good mixture:* If the group work is going to go on for a while,
  spend some time working the groups out in advance, so that you get
  a good mix in each one. Alternatively, an excellent way of creating
  'instant' mixed groups is by numbering the students. For instance,
  if you want groups of three and you have 30 students in your class,
  ask them to count around the room up to 10. All the ones will then
  work together, all the twos and so on. This works for groups of any
  size.

Chapter 4
Teaching and learning

What is this chapter about?

Teaching and learning lie at the heart of a teacher's role. However, it is only once you take on your first real teaching job that you realise the extent of the balancing act involved in getting learning to happen effectively. There is simply no way that you can be at your peak with the content and delivery of lessons at all times, despite what the managers/ inspectors might have you believe. You are going to have to make some difficult decisions in order to help you survive and succeed in the profession if you plan to stick it as a teacher for the long term.

This chapter gives you lots of hints about effective teaching and learning. It includes a range of ideas and strategies, including: why aims are so important; how to set up the pattern of your lessons; and how you might use resources to the best effect. In acknowledgement of the reality of a teacher's working life, I have also included a section that gives you ideas for how and what to teach when you are feeling exhausted.

Effective teaching and learning

Offering our children effective teaching and learning should, above all else, be an imaginative and exciting experience, both for the teacher and for the students. Sadly, the creative energy that you might spend on planning and delivering wonderful lessons often gets dissipated under the myriad strains of the job. Working with a tightly prescribed curriculum may also have a negative impact on your enjoyment of your classroom teaching. The tips below should help you maintain your enthusiasm for the job.

Stay enthused

As a trainee you had the energy and time to plan and teach some really high quality and experimental lessons. Although you may not be able to offer your children a constant diet of brilliant lessons, it is important not to lose your enthusiasm for the process of teaching. The positive reaction that you receive from your children when you teach a good lesson breeds more energy and leads to a much more positive outlook on the job.

Create and deliver engaging lessons

Working out how to get your children engaged in the learning process is an absolutely vital skill for the new teacher to acquire. A lesson that engages your class needs less energy from you in terms of classroom control, because your students will be too busy learning to misbehave. The positive response of children to an engaging lesson should also fire your enthusiasm.

Take a positive approach

Children are very sensitive to the vibes given off by their teachers. If you come into the classroom in a good, positive mood, planning to deliver an interesting and engaging lesson, this will rub off on your students and you will get a good reaction. If you feel negative about or bored by the lesson content and delivery, your children will pick this up and may well behave badly.

Use a clear structure

Children welcome structure – the teacher giving a pattern to the lessons and the learning. A good way to offer your children a clear structure is to state your aims very clearly right at the start of the lesson. Have a structure for the way that you start and finish your lessons, for instance with an engaging starter and with the children standing behind their seats before the lesson ends.

Set target

Students also like to have a target to aim for, whether for work or for behaviour. Set targets for how well the work should be completed; set targets that define how quickly an activity should be done; set targets for good behaviour too. These targets will give your children something concrete to aim for and a sense of achievement when they realise them.

Use plenty of rewards

Rewards go hand in hand with targets – if the children can manage to achieve 'x', their reward will be to receive 'y'. This constant target setting/ reward giving creates a sense of partnership between the teacher and the class. You are asking your children to work hard, and you are rewarding them when they achieve what you know they can. It also creates a sense of pace, energy and forward momentum in your lessons.

Don't believe the hype

As a new teacher you are going to have to get used to other people (usually those who are *not* in the classroom anymore) telling you how best to teach. If you sway with every fad and fashion that comes along, or try to pick up on every new buzzword, you will drive yourself mad. Learn to trust your own professional judgement, particularly as you become more experienced. Believe that *you* know what will work best for *your* children.

The importance of aims and objectives

I can remember my lecturers at university saying I should think very carefully about the aims and objectives of my lessons, but it didn't really make much sense to me until I actually started teaching. In recent years, the language around aims and objectives has changed somewhat, as is the way in education. Currently, you'll come across learning 'intentions', success criteria, WALT ('we are learning to') and WILF ('what I'm looking for'). But essentially, whatever terminology you use, these are all different ways of saying that you need to know:

1 What the children going to learn.
2 Why they are going to learn in it.
3 How they can show you that they have learned it/understood it.

On the next page are the reasons why aims and objectives are crucial.

They set boundaries for the learning

- This is what you're going to achieve during the lesson.

- And at the end…this is what you achieved.

They give a sense of purpose to the work

- This is the reason *why* you need to learn this particular thing.

- The children are more likely to approach it with a positive and hard working attitude.

They give specific targets for which the children can aim

- Just like setting a time limit for a piece of work, aims and objectives, set a learning goal.

- You can refer back to your aim during the lesson to keep the students on task and on target.

They create a sense of achievement

- At the end of the lesson, you can use your original aims to summarise what the children have done, and how well they have done it.

- You can discuss with them whether they have achieved what they set out to do at the start.

- If they have, they know they have learned something, and praise is in order.

They create a sense of a structure

- Having and communicating a clear aim encourages the teacher to be specific about what will happen during the lesson.

- The children feel grounded and understand the pattern of the lesson.

The 'organic' lesson

Having said all this, there is absolutely no harm in allowing some lessons to develop in a more organic way. Start with an interesting resource, or a topical theme, and see where the children want to take it, or what they'd like to find out. You might have some idea of where the lesson is heading, or you may simply allow your students to direct it in their own way. These organic lessons are probably best saved for when Ofsted inspectors are *not* in the building.

A model first lesson

At this point I'm going to give you a model for a first lesson to give you something concrete to hang on to. This is not model in the sense of a perfect lesson (in fact, you'll see the teacher make quite a few mistakes – see how many you can spot). It is a fairly static and 'safe' lesson, and could certainly be spiced up by incorporating some group discussions. What it does do, though, is give you a suggested structure to follow.

The model lesson in the box below is based on a first-year (Year 7) secondary school class. The class is doing a subject where written work is used, for example English or history. However, many of the points made and strategies adopted here will apply to children of different ages and studying different subjects. The majority of this first lesson is spent on explaining the rules and expectations. These are taught in exactly the same way as the subject content of a lesson would be delivered. You will see the teacher using many of the tips here that were given in the previous chapter on behaviour management.

The model is set out like a play script: I have included details of what the teacher says (non-italic) and does (*italics*), a commentary that explains the reasons behind her comments and actions (**bold text**), and also some possible student reactions with commentary of why the students might react in this way. I have assumed a lesson length of about one hour.

The model first lesson

The students arrive in dribs and drabs as they have had trouble finding the classroom.

The teacher does not feel this slight lateness is a problem in the first lesson with Year 7s and does not make an issue of it. This may be different with a class of older students who should know their way around.

As they arrive the teacher directs them towards the seating plan she has made and put up on the wall. They are to sit in alphabetical order.

TEACHER: *(to individuals and small groups of students)* Have a look at this seating plan I've made and see how quickly you can find your place. Well done Ahmed, that was really quick, you obviously want to go to break on time.

The teacher has challenged them to make the seating plan seem like a competition rather than a control mechanism. She has then praised an individual student by name (she knows his name from the position he is sitting in) to encourage the others, and hinted at a potential reward.

TEACHER: While you're waiting for everyone to arrive, you can chat quietly among yourselves.

The teacher knows that there is no chance or point in getting the class to be silent and then being constantly interrupted. It is far better to make them feel you have been generous enough to 'allow' them to talk for a while.

After a few minutes the students have all arrived and are seated alphabetically. The teacher has a copy of the seating plan in her planner, alongside the register. She now folds her arms and waits for them to notice that she is ready to start. They gradually fall silent.

TEACHER: Right, before I start I want to see *everyone* sitting still and looking directly at me. *(She pauses until she has their full attention.)* Thank you. Well done. As you know from your timetables, my name is Miss Cowley and I'm going to be your teacher this year. You can see how to spell my name, because I've written it on the noticeboard over there. *(She indicates the board and the students look.)* Now, in today's lesson we are going to aim to get through lots of administrative tasks: checking names, discussing our rules, giving out books and so on.

The teacher has waited for the complete attention of all the students. She has informed the class what the aim for this lesson is and why. She will refer back to her aim later, to ensure that it remains explicit.

TEACHER: The first thing I'd like to do is to take the register, so that I can check that everyone is here and learn how to pronounce your names. I'll also be able to check that you're sitting alphabetically, as on my seating plan. If I do pronounce your name incorrectly please let me know.

STUDENT: *(nervously calling out)* Miss, miss, I didn't realise we had to sit where you said. I'm in the wrong place. *(Other students start to call out that they're in the wrong places too.)*

The teacher should have stated 'Put your hands up if you think you might be in the wrong place.' She has also given rather a lot of information at

once and this may confuse them (see Chapter 3 'Give one instruction at a time').

TEACHER: *(Waits for silence with arms folded.)* Please put your hand up if you think you might be sitting in the wrong place. *(Thankfully only four hands go up.)* Now, one at a time please go and check on the seating plan where you should be sitting. You go first. *(They swap themselves around.)* Now, let's get on with the register. Ahmed.

As the teacher calls out each name she looks up to see the student and to check that she is pronouncing the name correctly.

TEACHER: Okay, well done. That's how I will start every lesson, by taking the register, so that I can find out who is here and also check if anybody arrives late. As you can see, I have a lot of names to learn and I'm going to need your help to do it over the next few weeks. You might be wondering why you're sitting in alphabetical order, well that's why, so that I can learn your names. Once I have learned them, and if I'm sure you are behaving yourselves very well, I might allow you to move to sit next to your friends.

The teacher has started to develop the idea of a partnership – they will have to help her learn their names. She has also explained why they are sitting like this, to pre-empt the question that would no doubt have cropped up soon. She has made it clear when and how she will allow them to move to sit somewhere else.

TEACHER: The first thing I'd like to do today is to explain exactly what I expect of you in my lessons. That way you'll be clear about what you should do and what you shouldn't do. If you have any questions at any time, please raise your hands rather than calling out, so that I can hear what each of you has to say. You're going to have to sit still and listen for a while, and I'm interested to see who's already good at doing that.

The teacher is now going to explain her boundaries to the class and she has referred back to the aim of the lesson. She has reiterated the point about raising hands to ask questions and has also explained why this is necessary. She has warned them in advance that they are going to have to listen carefully for a while and set a target ('who's good at doing that').

TEACHER: The first and most important rule in my lessons is that nobody talks while somebody else is talking. Can anybody tell me why this is so important?

STUDENT: I can, Miss!

TEACHER: *(Ignores the student who has called out and checks seating plan for the name of a student who has his/her hand up.)* Yasmin, you've remembered to put your hand up, well done. Can you tell me why this is so important?

YASMIN: So that we can hear what you are saying, Miss.

TEACHER: That's right. Very good. It's very important that everyone can hear what I am saying. You will also need to listen to each other very carefully. Now, what do you think the punishment will be if you do talk while I am talking Yasmin?

YASMIN: A detention, Miss?

TEACHER: That's right, but to show how fair and reasonable I am I will give you two warnings first, just as it says in our behaviour policy. After that, if you talk again I will have to keep you in for 15 minutes to think about your behaviour. If you still keep talking the detention will go up to 30 minutes. If you find it impossible to stay quiet, I'm afraid I will have no alternative but to send you to…(the head of department).

By ignoring the student who has called out, the teacher has made it clear that she does not want them to do this, without having to state it explicitly. After the student has answered correctly she has used praise and then repeated the rule, developing the answer a little (see Chapter 3 'Explain, repeat, explain'). She has then gone on to make the sanction for this misbehaviour clear. The sanctions stated will obviously depend on the individual teacher or school.

TEACHER: Now, my second rule is that you arrive at lessons ready to learn. That means on time, with your books and equipment, and in the right frame of mind to work. That way we can start work immediately. Put your hand up if you can tell me what you think you should do if another teacher keeps you behind, or if there is any other reason that you are late. Yes, Ben, what do you think?

BEN: We should get them to write a note in our diary, Miss?

TEACHER: That's right. Well done. And if you come to a lesson late without a very good reason, I'm afraid I will have to keep you behind to make up the time. Now let's talk about how we should approach our work. Does anyone have any ideas about this? Put your hands up if you do.

Although it appears that the rules are now being opened for discussion, it is fairly straightforward to elicit the responses you want or to mould the students' replies to suit your requirements. The teacher will continue to go through all her boundaries in this way until the class understand. It may be useful to write these down on the board as this happens. Setting boundaries may take about 10 minutes, but it is worth while. Another

approach would be to set this up as a group discussion, with the students contributing their ideas.

TEACHER: Now that we've gone through the behaviour I expect in my lessons, I'm going to give out the exercise books. When you get your book I want you to write the following information on the front cover as neatly as you can. *(She has this information on her whiteboard for them to copy: the subject; her name; the student's name and class.)* When you've finished doing that, sit quietly and wait for the next instruction. Any questions? No? Okay, who would like to volunteer to give out some books? Danny has his hand up and is sitting quietly, so does Claire.

The teacher has given clear instructions to the students and ensured that they get this right by using the whiteboard. She has also told them what they should do when they have finished – the students will complete this task at different rates. She has chosen to 'reward' the two students who are following her instructions by asking them to give out the books.

They give the books out. While the students are filling in the front cover the teacher walks around and checks that they are doing it correctly.

TEACHER: Now, before we start writing in our new books, I'd like to talk to you about how you should set out your work in them and how you should treat them. I'd like us to find about five rules to go in the very front. Can anyone put their hand up with an idea? Yes, Chirag?

CHIRAG: We should write as neatly as we can, Miss

TEACHER: Very good, Chirag. Jenny, can you tell me why you think this is important?

JENNY. So that you can read it, Miss?

TEACHER: That's right. It's very important that I can read your work, so that I can mark it. Before we put that rule in, though, there's something that we're going to need at the top of the page. Who can suggest what it is?

The student has indeed offered one of the rules the teacher wants, but before they write down this particular rule she wants them to say that they should always put a title and date at the top of their work. This needs to come first, as they are going to need a title for their list of rules. She has asked a leading question to get the response she wants. She can then write the title and date on the board and the first rule which will be 'Always put a title and the date on your work.' After this she can go back to Chirag's idea and any other rules she wants. It is useful to put rules about how to work at the front of an exercise book, so that they can be easily referred to in the future.

Once the rules have been 'negotiated' and written up on the board, the students copy them down while the teacher moves around the classroom and checks how they are doing. After a while, some finish their work and want to know what to do next.

The teacher did not let the class know what to do after they had finished. There are two options now: she could stop the whole class and let them know what the next task is, or she could let these few individuals talk for a few moments until the majority have finished.

After a few minutes it is clear that most of the students have finished.

TEACHER: Okay, I think nearly all of you have finished now, so I'd like everyone to look this way so that I can explain what I want you to do next. Anyone who hasn't finished can then go back to copying the rules down. *(She waits until she has everyone's attention.)* Now, I'm going to set you an exercise so that I can see what you are good at and what you need help with. Put your hand up if you can remember the rule I told you about what we do when we are working individually. Yes, Rizwan.

RIZWAN: We work quietly, Miss?

TEACHER: That's very good. You work in silence so that we can all concentrate.

The teacher now goes through the task she wants the class to complete, writing a title and the date on the board and questioning them to make sure they have understood.

TEACHER: Right, if you look at the clock you will see that we only have 15 minutes until the end of the lesson. I'm going to give you 10 minutes to complete this task, so that we have time to clear up at the end of the lesson. Are there any questions? No? Off you go then.

The students start to work, but one of them, Emily, starts to chat to her next door neighbour.

TEACHER: Emily, do you have a question that you'd like to ask me?

Roughly translated as 'I've checked whether the class had any questions and they didn't, I've told you we're not going to talk while working, so why on earth have you started chatting?' Combined with the 'deadly stare' this will hopefully persuade Emily to be quiet.

Emily becomes quiet, but a few minutes later she starts to talk again. The teacher moves alongside Emily and crouches down beside her.

TEACHER: Emily, I have made it perfectly clear that you are not to talk while you are working, so I am now giving you your first warning. Do you understand?

EMILY: Yes, Miss.

Emily becomes quiet again, but a few minutes later she starts chatting again to her friend, Jessica, who talks back to her.

TEACHER: Jessica, I can see that you've decided to talk as well, so I'm going to give you your first warning. Can you tell me what will happen after your second warning?

JESSICA: A detention, Miss?

TEACHER: That's right. And it would be a real shame to get a detention in your very first lesson with me, wouldn't it? I want you to get on with your work in silence please and stop disturbing the class. We have five minutes left everybody.

It is sometimes better to pick on the person who is being chatted to, rather than the one who is talking. This works because there is no point in someone talking if they are getting no response. The teacher has used this strategy and has made the sanction for ignoring her instructions very clear. It would be a shame to have to give out detentions in the very first lesson, but as it is almost time to finish, she will probably not have to do this. She has reminded the class about how much time they have left and will do this again as the time runs out.

A few minutes later.

TEACHER: You have one minute left now, so I'd like you to try and finish off the section that you are doing. When you have finished, please close your book and make a pile in the centre of your tables. *(A minute later.)* Okay, time's up, please stop and put your books in the middle of the table. Can I have two volunteers to collect the books in please? *(Lots of hands go up and the teacher chooses two students.)*

When the books have been collected in, the teacher stands with her arms folded and waits for silence. She has overrun a little and the buzzer for break goes, but she does not move. Eventually the students become silent, the more observant ones 'shushing' the others.

It is really important to have an orderly end to the lesson, as it ensures the students go away in a calm frame of mind. They will hopefully remember your excellent classroom control for the next lesson. The teacher is fortunate that it is break next, as the students are keen to go out to play. If it was not, she would have problems because she would be making them late for their next lesson. It is much better to end too early, rather than too late. You can always 'string out' standing behind the chairs by allowing one group at a time to push their chairs in and then practice standing in silence.

TEACHER: Right, as you can hear, the buzzer for break has gone, but I have a couple of things to say to you before we go, so can I have everyone looking at me? *(She waits a moment.)* Now, first of all I'd like to say that you've behaved yourselves well this lesson and we've got through all those administrative tasks that I wanted to complete – well done. However, next time I see you I want you to sit in alphabetical order again so that I can carry on learning your names. Secondly, at the end of every lesson with me I will ask you to stand behind your chairs. When everyone is standing still and silent behind their chairs I will dismiss you one group at a time. *(Some of the students go to stand behind their chairs.)* I don't believe I heard anyone say 'stand behind your chairs' did I? Please sit back down. *(She waits for them to do so.)* Okay, please stand quietly behind your chairs.

When they are all standing silent and ready she dismisses them, one group at a time, choosing the best behaved and quietest group first.

The teacher has praised the class to reinforce the behaviour they have learned. She has also restated the aim of the lesson so that the students understand what they have achieved. It may seem petty to make them sit back down, but it shows the class that they must wait for the teacher's command. By dismissing the best-behaved group first, she is making a point about who will receive the rewards in her lessons.

Eight lessons for the tired teacher

In your first term of teaching, you will be full of enthusiasm and energy, rising happily to the challenge of any problems that crop up. However, towards the end of the first term you may find yourself feeling both physically and emotionally drained. At this point I would like to offer a few suggestions for lessons which will give variety to your teaching and give you a rest at the same time. Although these are not lessons that you would use every day of the week, there is no need to feel guilty when you do need a bit of a break.

The important idea is that it is the students who should be doing the work, rather than you. Teacher-led lessons tend to be the most intensive; group work can be noisy; individual exercises tend to be the least stressful approach. This is not always the case, for instance, in the 'Show and tell' activity described below. These suggestions are not subject specific and you should be able to adapt them to your own area of specialisation or age range. The eight ideas are in the boxes below.

---

1. Look it up!

Give each child a dictionary or a textbook. Make this a competition to encourage an enthusiastic response. The children must look up the word or subject reference that you give them as quickly as possible. When they find the relevant page, they raise a hand. The 'winner' then reads out the meaning or passage to the rest of the class. If you have the energy, you can reward the children. One useful reward is for the winner to be given the chance to choose the next word to look up (this limits your involvement to practically nil). You can extend this exercise by asking the children to write down the definitions or passages into their exercise books. This makes the task longer and gives you more of a rest.

---

2. Time for a test

Tests are a good backup for when you are exhausted, because they involve no teacher input beyond setting the test in the first place (and marking it afterwards). The class has to work in silence, preferably for a whole lesson. The only drawback is the marking involved afterwards; adopt one of the marking strategies described in Chapter 6 to save time.

3. Time for the television

Although clearly you should avoid the temptation to show endless DVDs or television programmes to your class, there are certainly occasions when it is educationally justified. It is definitely a good way of having a 'lesson off'. If you are lucky, you may find a long DVD that takes more than one lesson to show. Ensure that the film links with the learning you have been doing and make sure you book the equipment in advance. If possible, set up the equipment before your students arrive, so that you are fully prepared and sure that it will work.

4. Private reading

Private reading works well with younger children but can also be successful with well-motivated older students. Basically, it involves them sitting in silence reading a book. You might plan this for a specific lesson each week, perhaps on a Friday when you (and they) are tired. The children could bring in their own books related to a topic you are studying. Make sure that you have backup copies as some students may forget to bring their own books, or may not have access to them. You might also allow them to read magazines or newspapers during private reading time.

5. A library (learning resource centre) visit

If you are lucky enough to have a good learning resource centre in your school, and a helpful librarian, you could plan some library visits for your students where you ask them to research information relating to their work. Alternatively, your library may run an induction programme at the start of the school year, and you could book your class into this. One of the basic rules of a library is that the children must be silent, so this is restful for you and for them.

6. Computers

Many schools now have suites of computers that teachers can book to use with a class, or a set of laptops that you can use. The first few lessons with computers may be stressful, but once they are confident about using the computers they will settle quickly to work and will happily stare silently at the computer screens, busily typing away. You can use the chance to visit a computer room as a reward, or build it into a scheme of work, so that you visit on a regular basis, perhaps once a week.

There is a wide range of learning that can be done on computers. In a maths lesson the children could learn how to set up a database; you could do graphics and design work in an art lesson; in a geography class the children could do map-based exercises. There are also many educational programmes available, for instance, to improve spelling. The internet also gives your students access to material on a huge variety of subjects. With older students, your school should hopefully block access to 'forbidden' websites such as YouTube and Facebook – check before you use the internet with your class.

7. Project work

Projects take time to complete and require the children to work independently. You could allow the students to choose their own activities for the project, or you could provide a list of tasks that they must complete. This works best with a well-motivated class, who are able to work on their own; projects can prove quite stressful if you have a class who are constantly going off task. You could combine project work with visits to the library and the computer room.

8. Show and tell

Although this is generally regarded as a pre-school or drama activity, it can be adapted to most subjects. A version of this is popular with very young children, who love to 'show' and 'tell' about something they have brought in from home. With older students, your show and tell could involve spending part of the lesson time preparing a presentation or performance which they then show to the rest of the class. This keeps your involvement to a minimum, and you will have the opportunity to assess their oral work during the lesson.

Dealing with differentiation

Differentiation is rather like close marking: all very well in theory, but not always practical for the hard pressed teacher. No doubt you will have explored some of the different types of differentiation while you were training, and tried them out with your students. However, now you have a 'real' job and all the extras that come with it: a busy timetable, marking to complete, reports to write, forms to fill out, parents' evenings to host, meetings to attend, and so on. Realistically, you will not be able to differentiate every task you set for each individual child, unless you are willing to plan and prepare resources until midnight every night.

On the other hand, differentiation is important, particularly for your least able children. If the work doesn't suit their needs, they are likely to go off task and start messing around. Here are some tips about how you can do your best with differentiation:

- *Focus on what really matters:* Focus your efforts where they will make the most difference – on the child who is really struggling because of severe special needs or on that small group of students who show a very high level of aptitude.

- *Get help from support staff:* If you work with a classroom or learning support assistant, elicit his or her help in differentiating the work. It could be that you create a worksheet then ask your assistant

to develop a simplified version for children who have difficulties
with literacy.

- *Plan for extension tasks:* A few children will always finish the work
  more quickly than others, so planning extension tasks is really
  important. When you plan, include a few more complex extension
  activities for those who regularly finish early.

- *Develop partnerships amongst your children:* Children are usually
  very good at working together and supporting each other. For
  instance, a child who has finished the work set very quickly could
  offer support and help to a weaker classmate. This is beneficial for
  your children's social skills and will also reinforce the learning.

- *Set differentiated homeworks:* For the most highly-motivated
  children, homework is a time when real progress can be made,
  because they can spend as long as they wish on the tasks. You might
  offer a selection of different activities for homework, letting your
  children have the choice of which to complete. Alternatively, you
  could specify who must complete the more difficult tasks.

When you consider differentiation, you might think automatically of
differentiation 'by task', i.e. setting different tasks for different children,
depending on their needs. Alternatively, you might focus on differentiation
'by outcome', i.e. by the fact that different children will turn out different
pieces of work even if set the same task. But there are plenty of other ways
to differentiate. Here are a few suggestions to get you started:

- Differentiate by time allowed – ask more able children to complete
  a task in a shorter time.

- Differentiate by target set – give a variety of targets increasing in
  difficulty, i.e. 'some of you could find 10 ideas, but I'm sure some
  of you could find 20'.

- Differentiate by support given – use any support staff both to help
  the least able, and also to extend the gifted.

- Differentiate by resources used – give some children an extra
  resource to support their learning, e.g. a dictionary, laptop or mini
  whiteboard.

Finding resources

Resources are brilliant for spicing up lessons, improving the learning that takes place, and making the work more engaging for your students. When you start at your school, check what resources are already available – they may save you replicating work that has already been done. However, you may find that they consist of outdated worksheets or textbooks that are difficult to access and impossible to use effectively.

Ask other teachers in your department or key stage if they have any recently prepared resources on the subjects you are covering. Teachers are usually flattered and keen to offer good material if you are enthusiastic and willing to give your own ideas in return. Look on the internet for resources such as worksheets that you can download for free. If you do make your own worksheets, present them as well as possible, as this will encourage the students to use them properly.

Remember that resources come in many shapes and sizes: a resource is anything that a teacher brings into the lesson to aid the students' learning. Children respond particularly well to unusual resources, ones which challenge them to use their creativity and imagination. Below are lots of ideas for original and interesting resources.

Objects

Children love it when a teacher brings objects, unusual or even common, into the classroom. They also love being asked to bring their own objects into the classroom from home. Objects are used frequently in science, art and technology lessons, but this is by no means the only time they can be used. For instance, an English teacher working on *Romeo and Juliet* might bring in the 'evidence' found at the murder scene. This would include the poison taken by Juliet, the Friar's letter to Romeo, and so on. The students could examine the evidence as detectives to work out what happened. In a languages lesson, you might set up a market in the classroom and ask the students to buy different types of food using the correct vocabulary.

In primary schools, teachers seem to use a greater range of props and objects in their daily teaching, especially lower down the age range. Here, too, objects open up a world of interesting possibilities. A jewellery box could become a magic object that holds the key to another world, but which can only be opened with the right spell; a selection of different hats or bags could help you in developing characters for a story.

The learning resource centre/ICT

Make full use of the school library and any ICT resources they have, such as cameras, programmable toys, the internet, and so on. Embarrassingly, you will probably find that the students are far more at home with the latest technology than you are. Before using ICT resources, get acquainted with the available material, so that you can organise what is going to be learned ahead of time. When using the internet, it is very helpful to create a list of useful websites, rather than letting your students waste hours surfing the net.

Other adults

Students respond very well to anyone who they perceive as an expert: a poet, a dentist, a company director, an engineer, a designer. Find out if any of your children have parents or carers who are willing to come in and do a session with your class, or ask around about ex-pupils who have moved on to successful careers. Other adults provide excellent role models for your students: a female bricklayer or a male dressmaker would challenge stereotypes and give your students something concrete to aim for beyond school.

In the primary school, teachers can make good use of parental offers of help, for instance, in hearing readers or in helping supervise a school trip. Make a point of asking the children's carers if they would be willing to give up some time to help you – you will probably find that they are flattered and delighted to be asked.

You might also ask whether any other teachers at your school are willing to swap expertise – an art specialist might come into your science lesson to talk about drawing, while you give the art class some information about human anatomy.

Other students

Some fantastic results can be achieved when older students work with their younger counterparts. You might find some sixth form students who are willing to come and assist you in a Year 7 classroom, or a group of Year 6 students to work with Year 1 children on practising their reading. This cross-school interaction is very helpful for developing many skills outside the traditional curriculum, such as socialisation and confidence.

Using displays

Classroom displays are an essential part of the learning experience for your children: they celebrate the students' work and provide information on a variety of topics. Although they take time to prepare and present, they are typically very worthwhile. These days, changes to teachers' conditions mean that, at the moment, displays are no longer part of your role. It might, however, be something you still want to get involved with – it is certainly a very creative part of school life and something that I've always loved doing.

Displays play an important part in creating a good working environment for your students. The children will respond far better to your lessons (and should give you an easier time) if they feel you really care about what they are doing and the place where they have to work. Displays can make the room feel like a happier and more positive place to be. When I visit schools to deliver INSET sessions, I can get a very good feel for what the place is like simply by looking at the type and quality of the displays on the walls. Consider the following suggestions and comments when creating classroom displays:

Change displays regularly

Where displays are torn, falling down or have graffiti on them, it would probably be better for there to be no displays at all. If possible, change your displays every half-term, or at least every term. Perhaps use a rota system where you always have one class or group working on creating a display and you take down the oldest or tattiest display to make room for the new one.

Avoid 'wallpaper' displays

Don't view displays as 'wallpaper' – something put up to decorate the walls (or to hide their condition). In some schools, as an open evening approaches, or as the arrival of inspectors becomes imminent, a frenzy of display work takes place (display work which then stays up for the rest of the school year). Students recognise this type of display for what it is: a promotion of the school rather than something done for their benefit. Display work should always be a celebration of what is *currently* going on in the classroom. It will take a while for you to fill your walls at the start of term, but this is not a problem.

Make it worth while

Only put up work that is worth displaying, perhaps because it is artistically attractive, because it is worth reading, or because it displays a particularly good effort by a weaker child. You might help weaker children redraft a piece for display if they have a problem with spelling.

Interactive displays

Aim to make your displays interactive and if possible three-dimensional. This encourages the children to respond to and interact with them. For instance, you could create displays with questions inviting a response, or displays that have lift-up flaps. There are many opportunities for creating three-dimensional displays: a model of the solar system for science, a set of masks for drama, a fireworks display for history work on the Gunpowder Plot.

By and for the students

It is tempting to put displays up yourself to ensure they are neat. However, displays will elicit a more positive response if the students have been involved in creating them. There is no reason why displays should not be created during lesson time.

Part of the learning experience

Treat displays as part of the children's learning – this will happen automatically if they are connected closely to the work the children are doing. Displays don't always have to come at the end of a topic or subject, as a demonstration of what has been learned. They can be used as a kind of 'working wall', which you add to or refer to during your lessons. Your displays might also include pre-printed material. For instance, a map of your area would be helpful for a class studying the local environment.

A motivating factor

There is something very rewarding about seeing a piece of work that you have done being displayed on a wall for everyone to see. By displaying their work you motivate the children whose work is on the wall, and also the rest of the class and other children who use the room, as well as pleasing any parents who visit your classroom.

Keep displays tidy

Whenever it occurs to you, take a few moments to tidy up the displays in your room, or delegate this job to the students. It is disheartening when students do not treat displays with the respect they deserve, but at least it shows them interacting with the work. By their very nature, displays become damaged as the students bump into them; accept the need to tidy them up on occasion.

Assessment

Assessment forms a key part of teaching and learning, both for the teacher and for the students. You need to understand the kind of level at which your children are working, and how well they understand the topic you are covering, in order to plan how best to teach them in the future. Your children need to know how well they are doing, both in order to stay motivated, and also to help them understand how they might progress further. On a different note, assessment information is also used to check how well different schools perform in relation to each other, and to see how much progress individual teachers make with their children's learning.

You can find lots of advice about formal assessment in Chapters 6 and 7, including advice on marking work and dealing with exams. Below are some general thoughts about assessment and the role it plays in your classroom:

- You will be assessing your students pretty much all the time – as you ask a question of the class and gain a response, or as you walk around the room checking books.

- These informal (and often subconscious) assessments will give you a feel for how each child is progressing.

- Encourage your students to understand what they are trying to achieve, and how they can go about doing this.

- Let your children know that it is a shared process – use inclusive language and plenty of rewards to keep them on track.

- Don't simply focus on academic achievement; remember to praise and highlight emotional and social success as well.

- Encourage your students to assess each other, and to share effective ways of working and improving.

Taking care of yourself

In many ways, teaching is like acting. You are performing to an audience of children, and you have to be in character as a teacher all or most of the time. There will be times when you do not feel like playing your part, but you have no choice – the students are there and waiting for your words of wisdom. This can become very tiring: after all, no actor is expected to perform on stage for five or more hours a day, every single week day. How can you prevent the inevitable tiredness that you will experience? Here are some ideas to help you cope with exhaustion during your first year:

Take your breaks
The temptation to work through break-time and lunch is incredibly strong and I completely understand why many teachers do it. You know that the work you have to do (and there is *always* work waiting to be done) will still be there after school. Why not try to get some of it done in your breaks so you can go home earlier? You may have detentions which have to be supervised, or students who need to talk to you about their work.

Try to be ruthless with yourself about taking your breaks. Aim to go for a drink in the staffroom before school starts, try to get there at break-time, and have as full a lunch break as you can. There are some very good reasons why you should do this. You need to let yourself rest during the day – you will not teach properly if you are tired and irritable. You also need to spend time with other staff: they are a vital part of your support system and there is little chance to get to know them unless you go to the staffroom. It is also good for you to have some adult company, a chance to have a laugh or a moan. Rest time is *never* wasted time.

Take sick leave
If you are ill, *do not* come into school. You are not indispensible, you do not want to pass on your illness to other teachers, you *can* afford to take a day off. Sometimes you know in advance that you are going to need a day off, for instance if you feel progressively sicker during the day. If this happens, and you feel you really have to, take some marking home with you to do while you're off.

Be a quiet teacher

A musician's tool is an instrument: it can be replaced if it gets broken. You voice is your tool and you must take care of it, because you only have one and it cannot be replaced. Avoid shouting as far as is humanly possible. Talk quietly, in a relaxed tone. Don't do too much 'chalk and talk' style teaching – make the children do the work as often as you can.

Make the most of your holidays

One of the biggest perks of a teaching job is undoubtedly the holidays. Use them for the most appropriate reason – to take a break. At the end of term you will feel physically and emotionally exhausted. Resist the temptation to catch up on all that marking and planning you never have time to do in term time. The job will expand to fit the amount of time you are willing to devote to it – you could quite easily work 24 hours a day and *still* not get everything done. Be ruthless with yourself and plan a proper holiday – you will feel much better for it when the next term begins.

Chapter 5
Pastoral care

What is this chapter about?

One of your key responsibilities, beyond delivering the curriculum, is for the pastoral well being of your children. If you're a primary school teacher, this pastoral duty will be for the children in your class. If you're a secondary school teacher, you will probably have pastoral responsibility for a form or tutor group. Although at times pastoral work can seem like one more burden to cope with, this side of the job is very rewarding. It feeds into the teaching and learning that you do, by helping you build up strong relationships with a group of students. This chapter gives you lots of tips and advice about the pastoral side of the job.

Your pastoral responsibilities

The pastoral responsibilities of the primary teacher or form tutor cover a wide range of areas, including administrative, welfare and social issues. Right from the start of term, you will be in charge of your children's overall welfare and their progress at school. You will have to do jobs such as taking the register, supervising the use of student diaries, helping children new to the school settle in, and so on. All this responsibility can seem quite daunting, but it is a very valuable and enjoyable part of a teacher's work. In some secondary schools, NQTs are not allocated a tutor group in their first year, or are given a co-tutor with whom they can work while learning the ropes.

First-year students

If you have a nursery or reception class, or a first-year (Year 7) form group in a secondary school, your main responsibility at the beginning of term is to ensure that your children settle in quickly and have all the information that they need. The following suggestions will help you prepare for the issues you and your students might encounter.

Helping the anxious child

Some of your children may need a lot of reassurance and comforting at the start of term. Starting at primary or secondary school can be a difficult experience, and you may be acting as a kind of surrogate parent for the first few weeks of the academic year. Keep an eye out for any children who are not settling in – this includes the quiet, withdrawn child, as well as those who display their anxiety more openly.

Finding the way around

First-year students will be unsure of the layout of the buildings, and will need help in orientating themselves. Your school should issue you with maps – work through these with your students. This has the added bonus of helping you find your way around. Make sure that the children know the location of the most important areas: the toilets, the class or form room, the assembly hall, the dining room, the student reception, and so on.

Understanding the school day

At first, the timings and arrangements of the school day will be very confusing for new students. They will need to be shown how the timetable works, when breaks take place, how long they are, and so on. One of the biggest changes for students starting at a secondary school is the fact that they have many different subjects, with a different teacher and a different classroom for each one. Spend time going over this with your form group right at the beginning of term.

Many schools have some kind of staggered start to the first term. In a primary school, the nursery/reception-aged children might start with half days before going full time later in the term. In a secondary school, the first-years might begin a day or two before the older students return.

Using a student diary

Many schools now use student diaries; the class teacher or form tutor needs to hand these out, get them labelled and explain to the children how to use them. Make sure you take a good look at a diary before the term starts, so that you are aware of exactly what is in it. Go through the different sections of the diary with your class, discussing how it should be used. Ensure that you give the students time to write or stick their timetables into their diaries, so they do not get lost. Form tutors should receive two copies of each timetable, one to give to the students and one for your own reference. Remind students regularly about jobs such as filling in homework sections, or ensuring that parents sign the diary.

Admin jobs

In theory, you should not be routinely required to take on admin and clerical-type duties, such as collecting money or chasing absence. In reality, there may be times when you do have to complete some admin jobs for your class or tutor group.

Finding out about your students

It can be surprisingly difficult, and time consuming, to get access to the information you need about your children. When I first started teaching, I had assumed I would get a folder with lots of details about my new form group. I soon discovered that if I wanted to get hold of information, I had to chase for it myself.

There are often confidentiality issues involved in being given specific information about a child. Your SENCO might be able to give you general advice about dealing with a child, but not be allowed to go into specifics.

Contact information

Your children, or their carers, will probably be asked to fill in a contact details sheet at the start of term. Alternatively, you may find that this information is written at the front of your register, or that the school office is able to give you any contact details you require.

Special educational needs

Some students will have special educational needs (SEN) and it is important that you find out about this as soon as possible. In the secondary school you could talk with special needs staff or with your pastoral manager. They should have access to material on the students from their previous schools (or, if they are not first years, from previous years at your school). In the primary school, the situation may be more complicated, as many special needs will not yet have been identified.

During the year, you may be involved in assessing children in your class for special needs. This assessment may involve making an initial identification of children who you feel are experiencing difficulties, or checking the progress of those with special needs by looking at how they are getting on in different subjects.

If you are concerned that a child might have unidentified special needs, don't assume that 'someone else' will pick up on it. Make a point of chasing this up yourself – too many children go through school with problems, without anyone ever picking up on it.

Child protection issues

There could be children in your class or form group who have welfare issues that are not connected to their learning. Find out as soon as possible who the designated Child Protection Officer (CPO) is at your school. This person is responsible for dealing with any child protection issues. If you do have concerns about a child in your class, talk to the CPO as soon as possible. Again, don't assume that 'someone else' will do it. Far better to highlight a potential issue than for it to get missed.

The register

The register is a legal document, and it is important that you fill it in correctly. Schools use a variety of different formats for their registers: the traditional green covered register, the computerised SIMs format, the handheld keypad system. Get some guidance early on about how to use your register. You may find that nobody offers to go through this with you – if this happens, please ask. Here are some general points about using your register:

Filling in the dates

The office staff should fill in the term dates for you in a traditional register. If not, you will need to do this yourself, but be careful not to make a mistake. Ask an experienced member of staff (or someone in the school office) if you are not sure. You should include half-terms and training days in your dates. If your school uses one of the computerised formats, there will be no need for you to do this.

Marking present or absent

When you are taking the register, a student is either absent (shown with a blank or an empty circle) or present (marked with a line). With a traditional register, check which colour pens your school wants you to use (probably black for present and red for absent). With the SIMs format, an HB pencil is normally used.

Absence letters, patterns and truancy

With changes in teachers' working conditions, you are no longer expected to chase for confirmation of absence from parents or carers. However, do still check that a child's absence is being followed up by the appropriate staff. This is especially important if you see a clear pattern to the absences, if you have general concerns about the child's ongoing health, or if you suspect truancy. Report any concerns to your Educational Welfare Officer (EWO) or CPO.

The register and assembly

Depending on the size and structure of your school, you will probably have an assembly with your class at least one day a week. You may be asked to take the register during this assembly. If you seat your students in alphabetical order in assemblies, it is much easier to mark the register. You can also work on learning their names: this can be tricky for secondary school tutors who do not teach their form group.

The student diary

Student diaries are a really useful way of communicating with parents, carers, or with other teachers. In primary schools this is sometimes called a 'reading diary' and usually goes in the child's book bag each night. Students can write down their homework and other important details in the diary; teachers can enter merits, detentions, general comments, reading tasks; parents can communicate with the teacher. The school will usually ask the student's parents or guardians to check the diaries regularly and sign or write in them. Here are some tips about supervising the use of student diaries with your class or form group.

Go through the format with the class

When you hand out the diaries at the start of the year, spend time going through them with your group. Look at the different sections, talking about what information should be kept in each place. Give your children useful hints about how best to use the diary, for instance, ticking or crossing off homework as it is done.

Check them regularly

Have a regular time when you check diaries, and stick to this. With a primary school reading diary, this might be as often as every day. In a secondary school, look over the student diaries at least once a week to ensure they are being used properly. This check up could take place during an assembly. Check the rewards and detentions pages, and ensure that the parent or guardian has seen and signed the diary. Give positive comments to any children who have lots of rewards in their diaries.

Use the diary as an early warning system

If a child is receiving a lot of detentions, find a time early on to talk to them about why this is happening. Is there a particular pattern of behaviour developing, or do they appear to have a problem with a specific subject or teacher? If a student is not recording homework in sufficient detail, or does not seem to be set much homework, follow up on this. If a parent is not using the reading diary, consider having a quick word to see if there are any issues with supporting the child at home.

Watch out for student tricks

Some secondary students will have picked up diary related tricks. Watch out for: diaries getting 'lost' when the detention pages are full; students who get themselves two diaries – one for detentions, the second a 'clean' one; forged parental signatures. To deter this, your school might charge a fee for each new diary, or you could keep a list of who receives one and when.

Contact with parents or guardians

Many primary school teachers, particularly lower down the school, will see the parents or carers on a daily basis, when they drop the child off at school. If appropriate, this can be the perfect opportunity to have a quick word about a child's progress or about any behavioural issues. If you prefer not to talk at the start or end of the school day, set up an appointment to meet at a more convenient time.

Secondary school teachers typically have little contact with the student's home, apart from through letters and student diaries. As a form tutor you may find that you only ever speak to parents or guardians on the phone, or when you meet them at parents' evenings. Your school may organise an information evening for new students, and this is a worthwhile way of meeting parents. You will also be communicating with them through subject reports.

Reports

The school report offers an excellent way of communicating with the home and of showing parents how and where the child is progressing (or not). In the primary school, the class teacher will be responsible for reporting on all areas of his or her class's achievement. You will need to comment on the different subjects being studied, as well as on the child's attitude, behaviour, and so on.

In the secondary school, one of the most time-consuming aspects of the role of a form tutor comes when reports are due. Tutors need to look at the different subject reports, and make an overall comment about each tutee's progress. Once again, new working conditions mean that you should not have to collate or proofread reports. If your school has a system where students take their own reports home with them, check that reports actually make it to the parents. If any children have proved particularly unreliable (or have a very poor report that they might not want their parents or carers to see), it might be best to post the report rather than give it to the child.

Social and personal issues

One of the most important (and satisfying) parts of being a primary teacher or a form tutor is dealing with any social and personal issues that arise. This can be challenging, though, both for the NQT and for the more experienced teacher. We want the best for the children in our care, and it can be upsetting if they are being ill-treated, either at school or in the home. Most incidents will, thankfully, be minor ones such as friendships breaking up or name calling (although these often seem very serious indeed to the child involved). Sadly, though, there are some children who suffer serious neglect or worse. Here are some tips about dealing with social and personal issues:

Get help with serious issues

Serious issues should always be dealt with in partnership with more experienced or senior teachers. If you have any suspicions about a child's welfare, refer the situation to your CPO straight away. There will be occasions when a student simply needs to talk to someone about something that is worrying them; use your judgement to decide when a higher level intervention is appropriate. If you are at all unsure, talk with a more experienced colleague about what to do.

Offer an 'open door' policy

At the start of your time with the class or form group, make it clear that they can come and talk to you privately if they ever need your help. In the primary school you will rapidly develop a very close relationship with each member of your class. If a child does approach you for help, try and make time to talk. If it is not possible for this to happen during tutor or class time, let the child know where you will be at break-time or after school.

Provide a shoulder to cry on

Often a student will just want someone to listen to their problems – a shoulder to cry on. You may find children come to you about friendship problems, or with minor worries about school or home. Sometimes, all that is required is for you to listen. If you feel that you cannot deal with the child's problem effectively on your own, or if you are concerned that he or she is perhaps depressed or overly anxious, refer the child to a school counsellor or similar.

Be a neutral observer

Give your group the sense that you care about how they behave in all their lessons and that you really want them to succeed at school. The secondary tutor can act as a kind of neutral observer, offering an overview of their behaviour or progress at school.

If a student comes to you and asks whether he or she can tell you something in complete confidence, you should never promise that you will not tell anyone else. It may be that a student reveals a child protection issue to you, and you will then have to break your promise.

House/year/vertical grouping

When I started teaching in secondary schools, year groups were all the rage; these days, many schools are reintroducing a house system, and some are using vertical groupings. The differences are as follows:

- Year groups – the children are divided according to their age (form group), and the year group team consists of all the tutors working together under a head of year.

- House groups – the children are divided into different 'houses', sometimes named after famous historical figures ('Raleigh', 'Drake', etc.). The house system allows for sporting and other competitions between houses. Primary schools will often have a house system running across the year groups.

- Year/house groups – A house system is 'tacked on' to the year groups, typically with a mix of houses in each form class. The house system is used to score things like sports events, merits and sometimes attendance.

- Vertical groups – Tutor groups are made up of students of different ages, in a 'family' style. This can help to create an atmosphere where the older children act as role models and as a support for the younger ones.

The role of the pastoral manager

In the secondary school an experienced teacher will work as head of year or house, managing the form tutors and overseeing the welfare and progress of a large group of children in one year or house group. Primary schools with several classes in each year or key stage will have a manager working as year group/key stage co-ordinator. You should refer any difficult or serious problems to this person – a written referral is more helpful than a quick chat during a spare moment, as the person then has the evidence required to take the matter further.

Do the best job you can with the pastoral side of your role, but be careful not to take on extra work that is not really yours, particularly as an NQT. You may wish to attend special needs meetings that concern a student from your group, as these give you additional insight into their problems, but there is normally no compulsion to do this. If you are experiencing severe difficulties with your form group, perhaps in maintaining reasonable behaviour, ask your pastoral manager for help and support.

Developing your role

In the primary school, because of your close relationship with a single class, you will probably find the curriculum and pastoral aspects of your work intermingling. It is a good idea to develop the sense of your class as a team who are keen to work and learn together, as this feeds into your classroom teaching. In the secondary school you will be spending less time with your tutor group, but you should still build a strong relationship with them. The following are various ways of motivating your class or form group and making them feel like a team.

Competitions
Organise a competition to see who can achieve the most merit marks or rewards, with a chart to mark the children's progress. There might also be whole-school competitions between groups for the best record of attendance and punctuality.

The class/form noticeboard
Maintain a well-organised noticeboard in your room, to keep your group motivated and informed. Encourage your students to help you design and update the notice board. Your noticeboard might include your name, the name of your group, a list of the school rules, names of the children in the group, their 'baby pictures', details of forthcoming events, etc.

Special occasions
Make your class or form feel special by giving them birthday cards, or cards to mark other special occasions such as Christmas or Divali. Make sure you remember to give every single student a card. You might also give out small presents to celebrate the end of term and if you're lucky you will get presents from the children in return.

Admin tasks
One of the most time-consuming tasks in a form group is getting them to hand things in, for instance return slips on reports and absence letters. Although in theory chasing these is not your role, you can help admin staff by motivating the children to get them back. You might give merits (or some other reward) to those who hand things in the next day; you could give out detentions for those who repeatedly fail to bring them in.

PART III

Climbing the Paper Mountain

Chapter 6
Paperwork and marking

What is this chapter about?

When you first start out as a teacher, you will find it hard to balance what goes on in the classroom with all the peripheral aspects of the job. This applies particularly to paperwork and marking. Dealing with form filling and marking books can take up huge quantities of your time outside the classroom, time that you may prefer to devote to planning or offering pastoral care.

For many new teachers, the paper-based parts of the job seem almost overwhelming. You find yourself using up huge quantities of time in a seemingly endless quest to 'finish' that pile of unfilled forms or unmarked books. Work is taken home on evenings and at weekends, and stress levels rise as your home life is affected by the demands of school work. The secret, as with much of teaching, is to find a balance that works for you and your children. This chapter, and the one that follows, will help you in the difficult job of 'climbing the paper mountain'.

Dealing with paperwork

One of the most time-consuming tasks faced by teachers is dealing with the mountains of paper that pass through their hands. Some of this paperwork is essential or very important, for instance, reports and SEN forms. Unfortunately, it is also true that the school for which you work, and the government of the day, will be willing participants in adding to your workload.

When dealing with paperwork as a new teacher, you may feel nervous about doing the wrong thing, or unsure of how to fill out a particular form. This leads to a situation where you put lots of pieces of paper in a 'to do' pile, rather than actually dealing with them. You then go through your 'to do' pile regularly, but you end up chipping away at the edges of it, rather than actually getting things done. You're going to have to be ruthless with yourself about this. As far as humanly possible, you should only handle each piece of paper *once*, using the four steps below to deal with it. If you find yourself handling a piece of paper for the tenth or twentieth time, something is going wrong.

Follow the four steps given below for each piece of paper, to keep your 'to do' pile to a minimum:

Step one: Deal with it *(straight away if possible)*
Step two: Pass it on *(so that it becomes someone else's problem)*
Step three: Recycle it *(someone else will always have a copy anyway)*
Step four: File it *(but only if you are definitely going to use it/need it again)*

Any pieces of paper left at the end of the four steps will have to go into that 'to do' pile for a later date. Here's a bit more information about each of the steps:

Step one: Deal with it

If it's a form, fill it in; if it's a training course you fancy, apply for it. Wherever possible give an immediate response so you can move onto step two. Don't agonise about what you're going to write far better to scribble a quick response than to put it in your 'to do' pile, where it will get lost under more important papers.

Step two: Pass it on

Once you've completed the paperwork, put it straight into someone else's pigeon hole if you possibly can.

Step three: Recycle it

If you can't deal with it and then pass it on, take a long hard look at the piece of paper and ask yourself: *'Does the thought of throwing this away make me want to cry?'* If the answer is *'No'*, recycle it immediately. If you make a mistake and throw away something important, someone else will always have a copy.

There are many types of paperwork that can end up in the bin. After reading the agenda for a meeting and attending the meeting itself, there is little point in keeping your copy of the agenda. If there is centralised documentation that is easily accessible, don't keep copies of your own. This applies to duty rotas, the less crucial school policies, the latest Ofsted guidelines and so on.

Step four: File it

If you truly need to keep the bit of paper for another time, and it would definitely make you cry to throw it away, then go ahead and file it. But be totally honest with yourself about whether it will be used again. Keep copies of photocopiable resources/worksheets in a plastic folder for easy access. File your resources in topics, schemes or year groups so you know where everything is.

A paperwork quiz

Let's do a quick quiz to see how you might deal with specific bits of paper you receive. For each of the following, have a think about the four-step process. Which of these would you deal with straight away? Which could then be passed on or thrown away? Are any of these things you would definitely want to file? And what about the rest? Just how big is your 'to do' pile getting?

	Step one: Deal with it	Step two: Pass it on	Step three: Recycle it	Step four: File it	To do pile
Timetable					
Payslip					
Survey					
Letter from the Head re. pay rise					
Admin form					

	Step one: Deal with it	Step two: Pass it on	Step three: Recycle it	Step four: File it	To do pile
Meeting agenda					
Message saying a parent has phoned					
Thank you card					
Child's exercise book					
Moderated student work					
Interesting article from your mentor					
Application form for training course					
Moderated piece of coursework					
Request from your mentor for your lesson plan for an observation lesson					

Marking: a balancing act

Marking is a job that expands to meet the amount of time you are willing or able to devote to it. On teaching practice, your timetable was only a fraction of that of a full-time teacher and you had enough time for planning and checking your students' work. Now you have to deal not only with teaching and marking, but also with writing reports, attending meetings, and so on.

Close marking takes a great deal of time. If you close mark a three-page piece of work, adding lots of comments and corrections, it could take up to half an hour or more. Multiply this by 25 or 30 students in a class, then by the number of subjects or classes you have to teach and you will see the extent of the problem.

To deal with marking effectively, you will need to:

- *Balance marking with other parts of the job:* Balance the importance of checking your children's work against the need to plan lessons, make resources, create displays, and so on. There are no hard and fast rules to follow, although it is tempting to feel that books must 'look' marked. Consider the value of different marking methods in terms of your children's educational achievement.

- *Decide on your priorities:* Do some skills/areas/subjects need to have priority over others when doing marking? At secondary level, consider which classes are most important at a particular time, e.g. marking practice tests for a GCSE group about to do their exams.

- *Maintain a home/work balance:* Realistically, there is no way that you can complete close and detailed marking at school. So, the question is how far you are willing to spend evenings and weekends finishing it at home. Don't let your work life take over your home life – you will not be effective in the classroom if you are tired and pressurised from working constantly outside of school.

- *Take shortcuts where you can:* You'll find suggestions for speeding up the marking process in the following sections ('Time-saving tips'). Don't feel guilty about using these.

When setting homework, bear in mind the maxim about eating doughnuts – 'a minute on the lips, a lifetime on the hips'. That piece of homework you set in an off the cuff way 30 seconds before the end of the lesson will live on for a long time when you have to mark it!

The marking options

Teachers mark work in a wide variety of ways, often depending on the age range and the subjects being taught. Experiment with different marking methods to see how effective you believe each one to be. Your school or department may have specific policies about marking that you should know about and follow. The three main methods are detailed in the box on the next page.

Marking methods

1. Tick and flick

The teacher puts a tick or cross on each answer and a mark or grade at the end. At the end of the work there is a brief comment, such as 'good work'. This approach suits a series of sums or a vocabulary test.

2. Close marking

The teacher highlights and corrects every single error. This is often viewed as the 'ideal' approach by managers and parents. It is, however, very time consuming and can damage a student's motivation.

3. Marking for specific errors

The teacher pinpoints one area for which he or she will mark, or looks at a specific aspect of the work when marking it. This could include the correct spelling of certain words (give a list out beforehand) or the accurate use of a technique learned in class. The teacher highlights some positives of the work, and is specific about why these aspects work well. He or she also sets a target for future improvement.

Pencil, pen, highlighter?

- *Pencil:* Pencil marks are easier to change if you make a mistake but they are harder for the child to see and more vulnerable to alteration. A pencil suggests a subjective rather than a definitive judgement of the work.

- *Pen:* Pen marks are easier for the child to see, but harder for you to change if you make a mistake, and less prone to student alterations. There's a stronger suggestion that the teacher is judging the child's work so this is more suited to a task with right/wrong answers.

- *Highlighter:* Very useful for identifying parts of the activity which work well or which need improvement. Easy and attractive for the child to look at.

Grading your students

Your school or department will have a policy about using marks, letters, numbers, national curriculum levels or comments (or a combination of these) when grading work. A final grade allows you to keep a record of how each child is doing. Consider the following points when grading your students:

- *Definitive marks:* Students and parents often like to have a definitive mark to show their attainment relative to others, and in relation to any statutory targets.

- *Comparing results:* With a definitive mark you can compare results between children and also over time. You might check each child's progress from one week to the next, or check progress across the class as a whole.

- *Grading across year groups:* In the secondary school, are you supposed to grade pieces of work in relation to the student, the class, or the year group? Is a grade A in a bottom set the equivalent to a grade A in a top set?

- *The potential for demoralising students:* Definitive grades can be very offputting for the weakest children. Give marks for both effort and attainment where appropriate.

- *Honesty vs diplomacy:* Balance the need to keep children motivated against the need for honesty. A series of low grades/levels may flag up for SEN staff that action is required.

Some time-saving tips

It's tempting to view marking as something the teacher does after a lesson, for the children to look through and absorb when the work is returned. However, there are plenty of educationally sound ways of saving time with marking, detailed in the box on the next page.

Time-saving marking

Do-it-yourself
The students check through/mark their own work themselves. Offer resources to support the less able (e.g. word banks or dictionaries).

Do-it-together
The whole class swaps work to mark a test at the same time. Very useful for right/wrong answers.

What's your opinion?
Volunteers collect in the books or papers and 'shuffle' them, then return them to someone else to mark. Give the students criteria for grading, for instance a mark out of 10 for creativity, accuracy, originality, and so on. Ask them to write a positive comment saying what they liked about the work.

What's everyone's opinion?
Get a second (and even third) set of marks and comments from your students by swapping again. This not only saves time marking but is also very educationally valuable for the students.

Marking in class
If you've incorporated private reading time into your classes, you may be able to mark some work in class while they read.

Setting non-written tasks
These are typically much quicker or easier to mark. For instance, ask the students to prepare a presentation on a topic during one lesson which you can watch and assess in the next lesson.

Collecting work

Always ask your children to collect in work done in lessons for you unless there is a specific reason not to do so. This saves you time and effort and they will be perfectly willing to help – you might even introduce this as a reward.

If space is tight in your classroom, ask the students to pass their books or papers along to the ends of rows, or to pile them in the middle of the tables.

Collecting homework

Collecting in homework can be quite a tricky administrative task as you need to ensure that everyone has completed it, and administer sanctions as appropriate. This is one time when it's best to collect the work in yourself:

- Before you collect in the books, ask the students to put their books in front of them, open at the page where they have done the homework. Go round the class checking that everyone has completed the task.

- Ask any students without their homework to have their diaries out in front of them so you can write in a sanction as you pass around the room.

- Consider when the best time is to collect in homework – this will depend on the class and age group.

- If you anticipate confrontations about uncompleted homework, wait until the end of the lesson rather than risk disruption.

- As an alternative, wait until the students have settled down to a long task, and then go around checking homework.

- Hand out rewards to those who have completed their work to a good standard.

- If you regularly have to chase homework, offer a whole-class reward when the whole class manages to bring it in. The power of positive peer pressure is often the most effective motivator.

- Consider having a 'get out of homework free' card as a special treat and a fun alternative to more traditional sanctions.

Keep an accurate record of your students' marks, so that when you come to write reports or attend a parents' evening, you have the information at hand.

Chapter 7
Exams and reports

What is this chapter about?

In this chapter you will find tips and advice about the formalised types of paper-based work and assessment. You can find information here about helping your children to prepare for and take exams, and lots of ideas on how to write reports. I also give a list of useful phrases for report writing that you can use to save you some time.

Exams and the NQT

Preparing students for exams is a rather daunting task for the NQT. There may be substantial pressure on you to get good results – from the managers at your school, and also from parents or carers, particularly if you are teaching in an academically successful school. The information, thoughts and ideas that follow should help you in keeping the nerves at bay, and in getting your children ready to do as well as they possibly can.

Statutory exams

Statutory exams are those exams which are taken by all children at a specific point in their schooling, and which are set and usually marked by external bodies. The government of the day decides on the stage at which these assessments take place. In recent years the trend has been towards an ever-increasing statutory assessment of school children.

Whether or not your children face statutory exams during your first year of teaching will depend on the age range you are teaching, and the age group or groups with whom you work. As you will see from the list below, a series of internally and externally assessed exams now take place at frequent intervals during a child's school career in England:

- End of Year R – Foundation Stage Profile
- Year 2 – SATs (teacher assessed)
- Year 6 – SATs and SPaG test (includes an external assessment)
- Year 9 – SATs (teacher assessed)
- Year 11 – GCSEs, NVQs
- Year 12 – AS levels
- Year 13 – A levels.

In addition to formal exams, many of the statutory assessments also involve a measure of teacher input. This might take the form of a classroom assessment that you grade; it could be that the students complete coursework or modular assessments over the course of the examination year. This aspect of statutory exams can add quite a heavy addition to your marking load.

Most schools include a set of school exams towards the end of the academic year. School exams can have quite an impact on your paperwork levels, as the marking load is often substantial.

Some tips on exams

Help your students get ready for their exams, whether these are statutory tests or ones set by the school. Although you should never 'teach to the test', it is only fair to help your students prepare to do as well as possible.

Preparing your students

Many children feel nervous in the run-up to exams – help them understand what to expect, and how to do well. The tips that follow will help you prepare your children for the big event.

Be well-informed

Prepare your children for the specific tests or syllabus they are studying. Spend time reading through National Curriculum requirements, past papers, mark schemes, and so on. Share these with your students as appropriate.

Get help if you need it

Don't be embarrassed to admit that you're not exactly sure what you are meant to be doing – better to ask an experienced member of staff for assistance than to muddle on and get things wrong.

Get acquainted with past papers

One of your top priorities, if you are teaching an examination year, is to look closely at the past papers (whether SATs papers, GCSEs, etc.). As you look at these past papers, think about how you will communicate the following information to your children:

- How the paper is laid out.
- The timing that applies to each section or question.
- The marks that apply to each question.
- Whether similar questions come up each time.
- The kind of wording that is used and what that wording asks the children to do.
- Whether certain topics tend to be repeated

Do lots of practice

Spend lots of time getting your children to take mock exams, either practical or written, depending on the subject. This is important because it trains them to work quickly – one of the most useful skills in an examination – and also because it will show them just how hard (and long) exams can be. Practice will help them learn to get the timing right. Help them understand that the examiner will give marks for each answer and if they do not finish the paper they will not gain any marks for the uncompleted sections.

Teach exam techniques

As an adult who has passed exams, you will know the best techniques for doing well in exams, so share this information with your students. Teach them not to 'waffle' or to give unnecessary detail. Encourage them to answer questions clearly and concisely. There is a great temptation for students to feel that the more they write, the better results they will get. Explain that this is not necessarily the case.

Teach memory techniques

Where the students need to learn sections of factual information, teach them the best ways of doing this. Tony Buzan has written some excellent books on memory techniques, and there is lots of useful advice on the internet.

Coursework

In the secondary school, external examinations may consist of both coursework and a final paper or papers. Here are some tips if coursework plays a part in the syllabus you are teaching:

- Approach your head of department for advice on how best to get coursework done.

- Check the deadlines for handing in essays or projects.

- Make sure the students and their parents are advised of these dates well ahead of time (your head of department should do this).

- Consider doing a formal check on work in progress, perhaps giving a series of dates to see sections of coursework, ahead of the final submission date.

- For those students who have difficulty completing coursework, remember that something is better than nothing. Find something to enter, even if they have not managed to complete a finished piece of work.

- As a back-up, set a mock exam in class on the coursework topic. Keep the answer papers, so that if a student does not submit his or her coursework in time, you can use the exam as a back-up piece.

- Students will often be withdrawn from the exam if they do not enter all the coursework required – let your class know this.

- Marking coursework, whether the first drafts or the final product, can take up a lot of time.

- This is especially true if you need to write detailed comments on the coursework to show how, where and why you have allocated marks.

How to pass exams

Passing (or failing) exams is often as much about how the student approaches the exam, as it is to do with the individual's abilities. It is tempting to assume that our children know how to approach and pass their exams, but in reality this is often not the case. Train your students in the skills they need to pass and do well in their exams. Here are some useful pointers about the type of training you might give:

- What to revise – which sections of the syllabus are most important.

- How to revise – making notes, memory techniques, etc.

- Any necessary preparatory work, e.g. for an art exam.

- How to use time effectively, both in revision and in the actual exams.

- Any skills specific to the subject, e.g. how to write essays, how to draw clear diagrams, how much working to show in analytical answers, etc.

- What equipment they should take to the exam – a pencil and ruler, a calculator, a copy of the set text, and so on.

Some tips on writing reports

Reporting to parents and carers can take many different forms. It can mean an informal chat in the morning or on the telephone, but it can also mean formalised written reports and parents' evenings. Schools use a wide variety of formats and styles for their written reports. Some use a computerised bank of statements for each subject, where the teacher can choose the statements he or she wants. Some use a combination of tick boxes or statements for specific subject skills, alongside a written teacher comment. Other schools require the teachers to devise comments of their own. The following dos and don'ts of report writing should help you understand the process:

Dos

✓ *Leave plenty of time:* In my NQT year, I was amazed to discover just how time consuming it is to prepare, write and collate reports. This is particularly so if you are a secondary teacher with hundreds of different students.

✓ *Be clear and concise:* Reports are not an essay written to please your college lecturer, they need to communicate information to a range of different parents and carers. Write clearly and simply so that parents can understand.

✓ *Make it look and sound professional:* The report is one of the main forms of formal communication between the school and the home, and parents may hang onto it for years to come. Ensure that your reports are as professional as your teaching.

✓ *Follow the rules:* Your school will have its own rules for written reports, for instance, that you should write in black ink rather than blue. You will probably not be allowed to use correction fluid on handwritten reports.

✓ *Strategies, targets and progress:* A good report includes strategies for improvement and specific targets on which the student should focus: words such as 'aim', 'ensure', 'develop' and so on are useful.

✓ *Focus on the positive:* Phrase what you write so that it will encourage, rather than demotivate, the child. Your reports for a difficult, chatty child might read: *'Although he sometimes tries hard, Johnny finds it difficult to maintain his concentration. He should work to avoid being distracted by other students.'*

✓ *Achieve a balance:* There will be times where you find it almost impossible to say anything positive about a student. A child who is proving this difficult to teach will be (or should be) receiving help from special needs teachers. The parents or carers, and indeed the student, will probably be used to receiving negative comments. Achieve a balance between honesty and subtlety.

✓ *Don't forget the personal:* Include at least one personalised comment on each report. Writing reports is not just about work, it's also about communicating your personal relationship with the individual child.

Don'ts

✗ *Get fancy with your language:* The recipients of the report will
   come from a variety of backgrounds and they all need to understand
   what you are saying. Avoid unnecessarily complicated language or
   technical terminology.

✗ *Be too informal.* Steer clear of slang and abbreviations – write in a
   clear, simple but grammatically correct way, using Standard English.

✗ *See this as a chance for revenge:* Even if little Johnny has been a
   nightmare all term, this is not the moment to get your own back.
   Avoid this kind of report: *'Johnny can't concentrate for longer
   than a few minutes and he ruins lessons by talking with his friends
   rather than bothering to work.'*

Shortcuts to writing reports

The date for reports to be sent home is usually written into the school
timetable, so try as hard as you can to hand your reports in on time. It is
very embarrassing indeed to have to admit that they are going to be late. In
the primary school, your reports will probably be checked by a more senior
member of staff, and you will be keen to make a good impression. In the
secondary school it is unprofessional if someone has to chase you for a set
of reports that should have been handed in the previous week. The names
of teachers who never file their reports on time will be well known in your
staffroom. Do not add your name to the list.

There are shortcuts you can take when writing reports, which should not
affect their quality too much. These shortcuts are particularly applicable to
the secondary school teacher who sees lots of different classes in one year
group. Balance your desire for parents or carers to feel that you are a caring
and efficient teacher, with the need to get the reports done in a realistic
amount of time. Here are my top time-saving tips:

- *Start well in advance:* In those secondary subjects where you teach
  many different classes, you may have to write reports on students
  you hardly know. This is particularly so if reports go out in the
  first term. Plan in advance for this eventuality and start preparing
  reports as early as you can. Do a few formal assessments so you
  have something specific to say about each child.

- *Use a computer:* If you have to devise your own reports from scratch, do it on a computer, perhaps using the phrases given in the section below. That way you can copy, cut and paste, and make changes really easily.

- *If you have to handwrite:* Always use a black pen, preferably one that can be photocopied without losing definition. Ensure that your writing is on the large side and that your signature takes up as much of the page as possible.

- *Use tick boxes:* If your school or department does not already use a tick box format, ask whether you might use tick boxes for different subject skill areas. You could then add just one or two comments on the end of the report, rather than having to comment on the skills in full.

Using 'types' of students

For the ultimate report writing short cut, use the following technique:

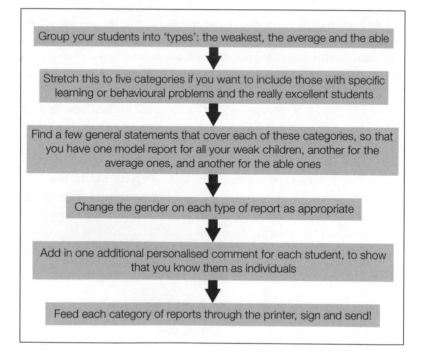

Remember, take care not to make any mistakes on your general statements, or you will have to correct/reprint the whole set.

Some useful phrases for reports

The phrases below give generalised comments about the sort of skills a student needs to succeed in his or her lessons, i.e. attitude, behaviour, concentration, etc. You will want to add your own subject-specific comments, for instance, on factual knowledge, reading and writing skills, analytical ability, creativity, and so on. I have grouped the phrases into the five categories suggested above, ranging from those with 'special problems' to the 'really excellent' students. I have also provided some personalised comments that I might use as appropriate and a model report for each category of student. In this model report I omit any subject comments, which you would need to include as well.

Students with special problems

Approach/attitude:

- Finds it very hard to take a positive approach to lessons
- Needs to develop a more positive attitude towards this subject.

Behaviour:

- Has found great difficulty in maintaining suitable behaviour in class.
- Must ensure that he/she avoids disruptive or confrontational behaviour.

Concentration:

- It is essential that he/she develops his/her ability to concentrate for extended periods of time.
- Must aim to focus on the task in hand at all times.

Co-operation:
- Must learn to co-operate with the other students in the class.
- Must ensure that he/she treats other students with respect.

Communication skills:
- Needs to learn to communicate clearly and effectively.
- Must ensure that he/she listens carefully at all times.

Contributions to the class:
- Must learn to contribute constructively to the class.
- Should always value the contributions of other students.

Homework:
- Is having difficulty completing homework tasks on time.
- Must ensure that homework is completed to the best of his/her ability.

A model report

John has found it very hard to settle into this class. *(Personal comment which hints at, rather than states, the fact that John is a difficult and anti-social student.)* Although he does try his best, he finds it difficult to behave well. John must approach his lessons in a positive way and treat other students properly. If he is to make progress in this subject, he must learn to concentrate better. John must also complete all homework on time and to the best of his ability.

Weak students

Approach/attitude:
- Needs to develop a more consistent approach to this subject.
- Should aim to take a positive attitude to his/her lessons.

Behaviour:
- Should aim to behave in an appropriate manner at all times.
- Is working towards improving his/her behaviour in lessons.

Concentration:
- Needs to learn to maintain concentration for extended periods of time.
- Should concentrate fully on the tasks set.

Co-operation:
- Should be more willing to co-operate with all members of the class.
- Should treat other students with respect at all times.

Communication skills:
- Should aim to make more contributions to class discussions.
- Needs to listen more carefully to instructions.

Contributions to the class:
- Should aim to contribute his/her ideas on a more regular basis.
- Must listen carefully to the contributions of other students.

Homework:
- Should ensure that homework is completed to the best of his/her ability.
- Must hand all homework in on time.

A model report

Candice takes a positive approach to this subject but her enthusiasm can result in a lack of concentration. *(Personal comment which suggests that Candice is normally a good student but can lose focus at times.)* She finds some aspects of this subject difficult, but is trying hard to improve. Candice should ensure that she treats other students with respect at all times. She should also make sure that she completes all homework tasks set to the best of her ability. This will help her to develop in those areas of this subject where she struggles.

Average students

Approach/attitude:

- Usually takes a positive approach to this subject.
- Has a positive attitude and should aim to build on this further.

Behaviour:

- Is generally well-behaved during lessons.
- Is a quiet and polite student, who always behaves appropriately in class.

Concentration:

- Is working hard to develop his/her concentration.
- Should aim to concentrate for increasing periods of time.

Co-operation:

- Co-operates well with other members of the class.
- Is willing to work in a variety of different groups.

Communication skills:

- Offers some ideas to the class and should now aim to be more confident.
- Listens well to instructions.

Contributions to the class:

- Makes interesting contributions to class discussions.
- Listens well to what other students have to say.

Homework:

- Always hands his/her homework in on time.
- Completes all homework tasks set to a fair standard.

A model report

Fred is usually a hard-working student who is always polite and well-behaved in class. *(Personal comment which suggests that Fred is a fairly good student who behaves well, but could probably do better.)* He tries his best even when he finds the work difficult and he always listens well to instructions. Fred should now aim to become more confident when contributing to class discussions and to complete all homework tasks set to the best of his ability.

Good students

Approach/attitude:
- Is a keen student who always takes a positive approach to lessons.
- Has an excellent attitude towards this subject.

Behaviour:
- Is always polite and well behaved in class.
- Sets a good example to other students by his/her behaviour.

Concentration:
- Can maintain a good level of concentration for extended periods.
- Shows good concentration when working individually.

Co-operation:
- Works very well with all the other students in the class.
- Is a co-operative student who always shows respect for others.

Communication skills:
- Always listens carefully to instructions.
- Offers some very interesting ideas in lessons.

Contributions to the class:
- Is always willing to make contributions to discussion work.
- Makes interesting and helpful contributions to the class.

Homework:
- Always completes homework tasks on time and to a high standard.
- Has produced some excellent homework assignments.

A model report

Kelly is a great asset to the class. She always approaches lessons in a positive way and shows a real talent for this subject. *(Personal comment that should please both Kelly and her parents/carers. It is always encouraging for a student when a teacher suggests that they have a 'talent' for a subject.)* She has worked hard to improve her work and is a keen participant in lessons. She should now aim to become more confident about contributing her ideas to the class. It is a pleasure to teach such a hard-working student.

Excellent students

Approach/attitude:

- Is a keen and conscientious student who is always willing to participate.
- Maintains an excellent attitude in every lesson.

Behaviour:

- Has maintained his/her excellent standard of behaviour.
- Sets an excellent example for other students in the way he/she behaves.

Concentration:

- Can maintain excellent concentration for extended periods of time.
- Demonstrates a high level of concentration at all times.

Co-operation:

- Is always willing to co-operate and help other students.
- Shows excellent leadership skills during group work.

Communication skills:

- Communicates his/her ideas in a confident and eloquent way.
- Listens very carefully at all times and asks highly perceptive questions.

Contributions to the class:

- Has made some fascinating contributions to discussion work.
- Is a very valuable member of the class.

Homework:

- Is always beautifully presented with a high standard of content.
- Has completed some impressive homework assignments.

A model report

It is a pleasure to teach Jasdeep. He is an extremely conscientious student and he is producing work of an exceptionally high standard. *(Personal comment that suggests just how good Jasdeep is at this subject and also praises his approach.)* He sets an excellent example for other students in the way he behaves and he is always willing to co-operate with and help the other members of the class. His homework is always beautifully presented with an excellent standard of content. He should aim to continue working as he has been doing so far. Well done, Jasdeep!

Some personalised comments

- … is always polite and hard-working in class.
- … is a lively student with a very positive attitude.
- … is a very valuable member of the class.
- … shows a real talent for this subject.
- … is keen, conscientious and always willing to help.
- … has a very mature attitude.
- … is a real pleasure to teach.
- … is a talented student who should aim to fulfil his/her potential.

PART IV

It's All About People

Chapter 8
Students

What is this chapter about?

Teaching is, at its heart, all about working with people. Your relationship with your students is at the centre of everything you do in your role, whether they are toddlers, children, young people, teenagers, or adults. In this chapter, you'll find lots of advice and information about dealing with different kinds of young people. There is information in this chapter about developing good relationships with your students, ideas for helping those with special needs, case studies based on a range of different types of student, and many other helpful hints and strategies.

You and your students

If you can create a positive and respectful relationship with each and every child, you should be able to encourage all your students to achieve their best. Here are some initial thoughts about the relationship between you and your children:

It takes time
It takes time to build a strong relationship with your children. This is especially so for the secondary school teacher with a large number of different classes and students. Don't expect miracles – it could be a year or more before some of your children come round to you.

Fear vs respect

In a class where the children fear the teacher, behaviour may well be controlled, but there is little chance of building a strong relationship. Aim to create an atmosphere of mutual respect between the children and yourself. However, be aware that you may have to persist with *giving* respect for a while before it actually gets returned.

A two-way street

You cannot ask for things from your students that you're not willing to give in return. If you want respect, show it; if you want co-operation, teach them how it's done.

You might not like them all

We don't necessarily like every person with whom we come into contact. Sometimes you may have to work with a student that you don't particularly like. Acknowledge your emotions to yourself, and then set them aside and learn to be a professional.

Dealing with the poorly behaved

Most teachers have to work with children who have behavioural problems, sometimes very severe ones. This year is about finding a balance between dealing with these individuals in the best way that you possibly can, and at the same time not allowing their behaviour to jeopardise the education of the other students.

Special educational needs

When you collect your class list or lists, you should receive information about any students who are on the register of special educational needs, or who have a statement. Find out, preferably before you start teaching, just what the needs are of the students in your class.

Don't prejudge your children

Don't have preconceptions about your children based on what other teachers say about them. Some children will be badly behaved in some classes or subjects, but will behave perfectly elsewhere. If you face the class already believing that child X will be poorly behaved, your expectations may create a self-fulfilling prophecy.

Personality plays a part

Although it's rarely spoken about, it's obvious that your personality affects the way that your children relate to you. If you are kind, pleasant and show that you like them, you will build a good bond. If you are moody, unpleasant and appear to hate them, you should probably quit teaching tomorrow.

Grouping the students

Different schools and subject areas use a variety of different methods for grouping their students, based on the intake, their educational philosophy and the age range in question.

In the primary school:

- The children are normally grouped by age.
- Same aged children may work in ability sets or groups for literacy/ numeracy.
- More able children may work with an older group or class for certain subjects.
- Sometimes, vertical groups are used so that children of different ages work together.
- In small primary schools, there may be more than one year group in a class.

In the secondary school:

- The tutor (form) or registration groups in each year will usually contain students of mixed abilities.
- These mixed groups may be put into different sets for some or all of their academic studies.
- Sometimes, these sets begin in Year 7, following an initial test or screening.
- Some schools work with mixed ability classes to start with, then put the children into ability sets in Year 8 or above.

- In some subjects, most classes will be mixed ability, with only a 'top' and 'bottom' set at either end of the ability range.

- Although less common these days, some schools 'stream' their students, creating two different ability groups within a year (in the past these may have been untactfully called the 'A' and 'B' streams).

There is much discussion about whether students are better served by setting, streaming or by mixed ability teaching. You will come to your own conclusions about this, but in reality you will have little influence on the creation of groups until you gain promotion. The following comments are based on my own experience of teaching different groupings of students. They cover the advantages and disadvantages of these for the teacher, rather than taking a philosophical perspective on the subject.

Teaching top sets and high ability students

Advantages:

- ✓ It is very enjoyable to teach a group of highly-motivated and intelligent children.

- ✓ They stretch you intellectually and there are usually fewer discipline problems.

- ✓ You will move quickly through the work and you can try out some more creative strategies.

- ✓ There is usually little need to differentiate the work you set.

- ✓ You get to stretch your own subject knowledge and to revel in a subject at a higher level.

Disadvantages:

- ✗ Your marking load will be heavy, as these students are likely to work at a fast pace.

- ✗ You will need to be on top of the subject in order to field any awkward questions.

- ✗ You may also encounter ambitious parents who question the quality or quantity of your teaching.

- ✗ Students in top sets (or with high ability levels) can sometimes become arrogant or lazy because they feel that they 'know it all' already.

✗ It can be difficult to know how best to discipline them for this behaviour.

Teaching mixed ability groups

Advantages:

✓ There is typically a good and interesting mix of characters in a mixed ability group.

✓ The stronger children can encourage the weaker ones to achieve better results.

✓ The children are generally fairly well motivated.

✓ You will not have quite the marking load that you would have with a top set.

Disadvantages:

✗ If there are disaffected children in a mixed-ability group, they can affect the quality of the lesson for the more able or well-motivated students.

✗ This can cause tensions within the class between those who want to learn and those who do not.

✗ You will have to differentiate the work you set if there is a wide range of abilities in the class.

Teaching bottom sets and lower ability students

Advantages:

✓ If you teach a bottom set, or a group of weak students, your marking load is fairly small.

✓ You can keep well ahead of the children in your planning.

✓ Often bottom sets are deliberately designed to contain a smaller number of students.

✓ You can use highly structured lessons and even try out some more unusual strategies that could appeal to these children.

✓ You may well have support teachers or assistants to help you.

Disadvantages:

✗ If the children have behavioural problems, you might experience some more serious confrontations.

✗ If they are not willing to work hard you are going to have to find ways to encourage them to improve.

✗ With this type of group you are not intellectually stretched by the lessons you are teaching.

✗ You may find this type of group physically and psychologically tiring to work with.

✗ There can be a tendency to place children who have behavioural issues in these sets as a matter of course rather than because of aptitude.

✗ For those children with behaviour issues but with high academic ability this can lead to frustrations and consequently to a worsening of behaviour.

Special educational needs

The special needs teachers at your school have a great deal of expertise in this subject, and you should always refer to them for help and advice. This section gives a brief introduction to some common types of special educational needs, as well as some tips on accessing the information you need and on dealing with SEN related behavioural problems.

Special educational needs – a quick guide

There are a huge range of different types of special need, with new conditions being identified, recognised and named all the time. The types of special educational needs that you are most likely to come across are outlined below.

Social, emotional and behavioural difficulties

This is usually abbreviated to EBD or SEBD. The term covers a wide range of problems – confrontational behaviour, the withdrawn child, the 'school refuser', and so on.

ADHD

This stands for Attention Deficit Hyperactivity Disorder. Some children with this problem do not have hyperactivity and will be described as having 'ADD'. These students find it very hard to focus, concentrate, stay still, make eye contact, and so on.

Specific learning difficulties

Often abbreviated to SpLD. This covers a range of problems which are usually obvious in one area of the curriculum or within one skill area. For instance, a child might have a problem with communication, or with motor skills (dyspraxia).

Dyslexia

This term is often used (wrongly) to describe any problems with spelling, writing and so on. Simply put, dyslexia describes a problem with recognising words. If you notice a child who often puts letters the wrong way round, or in the wrong order, but she is generally able, this might indicate that he or she has dyslexia. Find out more about the subject by visiting www.dyslexiaaction.org.uk.

English as a second language / English as an additional language

These two terms, abbreviated to ESL and EAL, describe those students for whom English is not their first language. They might speak another language at home and this could cause them difficulties in their lessons. These students will need support with grammatical constructions and with new or technical terminology.

Accessing records

Get to know the people involved with SEN in your school as soon as possible. They can advise you on dealing with students who have difficulties and will help you understand the causes of poor behaviour from specific individuals. They can tell you about the learning needs of certain children and help you match your lesson content and delivery to these needs. The information may well come in the form of an Individual Education Plan (IEP) or other similar format. The IEP will identify strategies, targets and so on.

Bear in mind that some aspects of a child's records may be confidential, but you should still be able to gain a general idea of what is going on. Again, though, I would stress that you should not prejudge your students on this material, merely use it to inform your teaching and learning approaches.

Dealing with behavioural problems

Children who have special needs often become frustrated in the classroom, because they find it difficult to access the learning. This can lead to behavioural issues as the child tries to deflect attention from his or her problem. Make sure that you differentiate appropriately for those students with SEN. If you teach a child who has serious behaviour problems, look carefully at the ideas given in Chapter 3. Below are a few additional tips.

Isolate the troublemaker

Every attention-seeker wants an audience so isolate the child to stop the behaviour problem from spreading. Take him aside to talk quietly rather than getting into a confrontation in front of the whole class.

Get down to their level

It is much easier to reason with someone if you are *literally* on the same level as them. Crouch down beside a student to chat.

Remain reasonable at all times

Or, in other words, *you're the adult*. Remain calm no matter how hard it is, modelling appropriate behaviour for the child. For some children, adult role models at home use an aggressive approach. Refuse to shout or get angry, and eventually the student will learn to trust you.

Keep your voice low and quiet

This calms the situation down and forces the child to slow down and consider their behaviour. It also stops you from becoming a loud teacher and wearing out your voice.

Explain the problem

Often a young child will not understand why their behaviour is inappropriate, so explain what the problem is and what the child could do about it. Encourage your students to *change* their behaviour, rather than always *managing* it yourself.

Stick to your guns

Back to those boundaries again! You are the teacher, you have set the rules and have been fair and clear about it. Do not give in to pacify a child. If you do, you are storing up trouble for yourself in the future.

State the sanction clearly

Staying calm and reasonable, inform the child of what will happen if the misbehaviour continues. The student (and the class) should see you sticking to your boundaries as much of the time as you can.

Depersonalise the sanction

You don't want the child to feel that he or she is receiving a personal reprimand, so try to depersonalise the punishment by saying: *'Unfortunately, if you continue to [state misbehaviour] you will force me to [state sanction].'*

Talk about choices

Frame what you say in terms of choices. Describe the good or 'right' choice, and the positive benefits of doing this. Describe what you will have to do if the student chooses to continue to misbehave.

Case studies

The fictitious case studies below reflect a variety of situations you may face in your NQT year. The case studies give details about the student, what the problem is, and some ways in which you could deal with it. Much of how you deal with real-life problems depends on the situation you find yourself in, the type of class you have and the child's reactions to what you do and say. These case studies should provide a useful starting point from which to work during your NQT year.

The 'odd-one-out'

The student

Joe is rather a strange child. He lacks social skills and does not integrate well with the rest of the class. If you are honest, you can understand why they do not want to work with him. His behaviour is strange and he can become quite confrontational if the other children do not accept his ideas.

At the start of term, the students were willing to work with Joe, but as time goes on they are becoming increasingly frustrated by him and keep asking you not to make them work with him. You are becoming worried about what might happen if someone refuses point blank to co-operate.

Dealing with the problem

1 Find out whether Joe is on the SEN list. If he is, ask for some more information about exactly what his problem is and what strategies you should use with him. If he is not on the list, highlight your concerns with the SENCO.

2 Take Joe to one side after a lesson and ask him if he feels he is settling in okay and if not, why not. Offer him some strategies to help him get on with the other students better, for instance, making eye contact and respecting other people's ideas.

3 At the start of the term you will have set the boundaries and *all* the students must follow them. If any children refuse to work with Joe, simply state to them that they must respect the others in the class by working in the groupings you have organised. Follow the appropriate sanctions if anyone refuses.

4 Another option is to 'fix' the groups to avoid any potentially tricky combinations. This avoids the possibility of confrontation, although you are not really addressing the root of the problem.

5 If it fits in with your subject/age group, do some work on the topic of 'making friends' with the class, in the hope that Joe will pick up some tips.

The potentially violent student

The student

Thelma is well known around the school for her violent temper, which flares up out of the blue. She is usually a fairly well-motivated student and she has produced some good work for you. However, she does have a tendency to argue with a couple of the other children in your class.

At the moment these arguments are only verbal, but they are getting increasingly vicious. You worry that they might escalate into physical violence. You can sense a lot of tension building up in the class.

Dealing with the problem

1 Check whether the SEN staff have identified any specific behavioural difficulties. Ask for their advice on how you should deal with her – they may know about specific events or actions that make her temper flare up.

2 Talk to Thelma individually about her behaviour and try to help her work out what it is that makes her angry and how she might deal with it in an appropriate way. Encourage her to develop empathy, helping her understand how others perceive her behaviour.

3 Teach Thelma some relaxation and anger management techniques, for instance advising her to count down from 10 when she feels herself getting upset.

4 Move Thelma to sit away from any children who might be pulled into an argument with her. If possible, sit her on her own at a desk near the front of the room. If she becomes confrontational when asked to do this, explain that you are trying to help her control her temper.

5 When Thelma does get into confrontations, defuse the situation by talking to her quietly, moving her away from the person she is quarrelling with, or by asking her to step outside to calm down (perhaps with a friend).

6 If a violent confrontation seems likely to take place, remove Thelma from the classroom as quickly as possible. Offer her the option of going to sit in a quiet and private area when she feels herself about to blow.

The student with poor concentration

The student

Fred generally behaves well in class, but he has a problem finishing work. His confidence in his work is very low and he rarely concentrates long enough to complete anything. He complains of tiredness if you ask him to write for more than a few minutes at a time.

Fred's work is often very difficult to read and he has now started to distract other students nearby, chatting to them when he runs out of steam. He very rarely completes his homework.

Dealing with the problem

1   Talk to the SEN staff about whether Fred has a specific learning difficulty of some kind. This might also explain the poor presentation of his work – perhaps he is hiding the fact that he cannot spell or perhaps he does not understand the work you are doing.

2   Give Fred small but achievable targets for his written work. Draw a line half-way down the page and ask him to write to that point. Set him a target to write a specific number of words.

3   Talk to him about why it is important for him to work neatly and complete the tasks set. Ask him if there is a problem that you can help him with.

4   Stick to the boundaries you have set for the class – sanction Fred for uncompleted homework and for chatting in lessons, to encourage him to concentrate.

5   Consider phoning Fred's parents or carers to talk to them about his homework. This often helps by identifying that this is a problem and showing the child that you want to solve it. Are his parents able to support him at home with completing his work?

6   Fred may find it helpful to work on a computer, as it is possibly the act of writing that is tiring him. If your school has a laptop, let him use it as a reward for sustained focus in lessons.

The arrogant student

The student

Sandra is a very self-confident student, but her confidence often comes across as arrogance. She completes all the work you set to a high standard, but she has started pushing at the boundaries, for instance, interrupting when you are talking to the class.

Sandra is frequently late for class, and when you ask her where she has been, she always has some sort of excuse, but nothing to back it up. You believe she is lying to you. Whenever you challenge her behaviour, she says your lessons are boring and she doesn't enjoy them. She frequently says (out loud to the class) that Mr Evans, the teacher they had last year, was much better than you. She asks you repeatedly if you are a new teacher.

Dealing with the problem

1   Stick rigidly to your boundaries, but in a calm way. When Sandra oversteps the mark, apply the appropriate sanction. Explain to her that being late without a note means that she will receive a punishment, just as it would for any other member of the class.

2   When a student says your lessons are boring, it's tempting to respond to the accusation. You may not feel particularly confident yet about what you are teaching and Sandra seems to sense this. Either ignore the comments, simply pretending not to hear them. Alternatively, surprise her by taking the opposite tack, and saying: *'I know, isn't it terrible? I've tried everything I can think of but still I can only dream up these really boring lessons. Perhaps you could help me by planning part of the next one for me?'* Do this without any hint of sarcasm in your voice.

3   If it seems appropriate, talk to Sandra about her behaviour and explain why it is unacceptable. You might ask a more senior or experienced teacher to have a word with her as well, but be wary of undermining your own authority.

4   Try flipping things round, and getting Sandra to contribute to lesson delivery. She seems an able and confident student, so encourage her to participate during lessons, for instance by writing up answers on the board for you.

The unhappy or shy student

The student

Selina is a quiet, well-behaved child. She rarely puts her hand up in class, but she always completes her work quickly and neatly. You have heard the other students referring to her as a 'boffin' and laughing at her glasses.

She doesn't seem to have any friends in class and you often see her wandering around the school alone at break and lunch-time. Recently she has become even more withdrawn in lessons.

Dealing with the problem

1 It seems possible, from the information here, that Selina is being bullied. In the secondary school, talk to Selina's form tutor to see whether this is a possibility. In the primary school, keep an eye out to see whether there are incidents of bullying taking place around school, asking a playground supervisor to do the same at play times.

2 Have a chat to Selina about what is wrong. Perhaps she came from a different school or area to all the other children and does not know anybody? You could mention that you have noticed that she is very quiet in class and ask her whether she wants to talk to you about anything.

3 Try every way you can to improve Selina's self-confidence. Praise her work, but in written comments rather than in front of the class, to avoid the others developing the notion that she is a 'boffin'. Encourage her to become more of a participant in class discussions, but don't force her to answer questions in front of her peers.

4 Ask the appropriate pastoral manager whether you can contact Selina's parents or guardians to set up a meeting. They might not realise that Selina is finding school so hard or may have similar concerns. You can work together to try to resolve the situation.

5 Encourage some of the more sensitive children to include her in their break and lunch-time activities. Suggest to Selina that she joins a homework club or other break time activity, so that she has somewhere to go and the opportunity to make friends.

The verbally aggressive student

The student

Colin is an extremely difficult student with severe emotional and behavioural difficulties. He claims that you pick on him and whenever you try to tell him off or ask him to complete work he reacts badly, throwing abuse at you. The standard of his written work is very poor and he rarely finishes anything.

Colin is also confrontational with the other children and none of them want to work with him. Your class has quite a few difficult children in it and you feel that Colin is dragging them all down with him.

Dealing with the problem

1 Try to find out the background to Colin's problems so that you can avoid exacerbating the situation: perhaps it is something specific that sets him off. Ask special needs staff for advice on how to deal with him and ask for extra support in your classroom.

2 Be as fair and firm as you can, sticking closely to the boundaries you have set and explaining why his behaviour warrants the sanctions you give. Make it clear that, rather than the sanction being your choice, it is his choice because of the way he is behaving.

3 At times you may need to flex your boundaries a little with Colin, depending on how severe the problem is. This might mean overlooking minor infringements for the first bit of the lesson, until he is settled and calm.

4 Use praise as much as you can: whenever you see Colin doing something positive, commend him for it. It is easy to slip into negative responses with very challenging children. Bear in mind that this child has severe problems, so try not to take what he says or does personally.

5 Put Colin in a group with some of your best students, those who will not respond to any disruptive behaviour and who will hopefully motivate him. Use careful praise of these children to encourage Colin to emulate them. Offer some really good rewards to the whole class and aim to give one to Colin.

6 Telephone or meet with his parents or carers (preferably before the parents' evening, if it is not early on in the year). Check first with the special needs staff to ensure that this is okay. A chat with his parents could give you an insight into his behaviour.

Chapter 9
Staff

What is this chapter about?

Teaching attracts a diverse range of people, of all different personality types. Some of the staff at your school would have started out on their careers long ago, others will be young teachers or new to the profession, just like you. A large secondary school may have a hundred teachers or more, plus lots of other staff including science technicians, office staff and catering workers. Even if you work in a small primary school, there will still be a range of teaching and non-teaching staff working together in the staff team.

In some schools, the staff work well together and there are very few tensions. In other schools, staffroom politics and personal rivalries create a difficult atmosphere. You will come across some teachers who seem cynical and disillusioned with the job, and others who enthuse about it and approach their work with passion. In this chapter you will find lots of tips about working with the other members of staff at your school. You'll find suggestions about who it is useful to get to know, as well as some light-hearted thoughts about different 'types' of teachers. You'll also find plenty of ideas about working with support staff, and coping with the foibles of senior management.

Getting to know the right people

School staff are, on the whole, brilliant at supporting and helping each other. Make it a priority, early on in your induction year, to get to know as many people as you can. Wear a smile and always say hello to other members of staff as you pass around the school (no matter how stressed you are feeling). Don't just focus on getting to know the other teachers – be as friendly with the caretaker as you are with your induction tutor. Doing this has a number of advantages:

- You become a member of the school team.
- These other people will help and support you.
- In return, you can be helpful and supportive to them.
- It's part of your professional role and of gaining qualified teacher status (QTS).
- Getting on with other staff in your job will make your working life much easier and happier.
- Those who've been in the job for a while are a great source of practical tips and advice.
- They can also advise you about some of the less positive aspects of the job, for instance dealing with paperwork.

Useful people to get to know

- Experienced teachers (but not the cynical ones).
- Advanced skills teachers.
- Your induction tutor.
- The union representatives.
- Heads of department (of subjects other than your own).
- Curriculum co-ordinators.
- Support staff.
- Office staff.
- Buildings and maintenance staff.
- The caretaker.

- The cleaners who clean your room.
- Caterers/lunchtime supervisors.
- Volunteers.
- SEN staff.
- The school SENCO.
- The LRC manager (head librarian).
- The head's secretary.

Getting to know the wrong people

Unfortunately, there may also be people in your school who you should avoid like the plague. These are the people who have stayed in teaching because they cannot (or cannot be bothered to) get another job. To them, teaching is not a vocation but an irritation. They will moan at every opportunity and to anyone who will listen about how dreadful the students are. Teaching is, of course, a tough job, and I would never try to deny that. However, the only way to give the students a fair deal and to enjoy it is to work hard at it. Try to avoid those teachers whose cynicism and jaded attitudes might wear you down.

Types of teachers

The examples that follow are fictitious, a bit stereotyped and, hopefully, amusing. Teachers are individuals and use a mixture of styles in the classroom, depending as much on the class as on their personality. However, you might like to see if you can recognise any of these teachers in your own school. You might also like to keep a watch out for any of the negative traits developing in your *own* teaching style.

The 'old-school-tie' teacher

Dress code: Always dresses smartly and, if male, wears a suit and tie; this teacher believes school uniform is vital for maintaining discipline amongst the children.

Favourite catchphrases: Sentences starting with *'In my day...'*, for instance, *'In my day children knew how to behave themselves.'* The question *'Would you do that at home?'* is used for various misdemeanours. *'You boy/girl!'* is shouted to gain a child's attention.

Discipline code: A strict disciplinarian who believes that children or pupils (never students or young people) should be seen and not heard.

Favourite method of discipline: Would like to use the cane, but since this is no longer allowed, gives the children a verbal thrashing instead. Keen on giving out vast quantities of lines and lots of detentions. Likes to send children to stand outside the classroom, where they are immediately forgotten about until the inspector/headteacher arrives.

Teaching style: A strong focus on traditional methods and working in silence. No exploratory, creative or group work.

Marking strategy: A red pen is used to put lots of crosses, a few ticks, and a mark out of ten on each piece of work.

Bad habits: A tendency to turn red and spit when angry. The male of the species has a poor taste in ties. Likes moaning out loud in the staffroom.

Classroom layout: Desks in rows, facing the teacher.

Condition of teacher's desk: Very neat, with only one pile of marking to be done and lots of red pens to use when doing it. Do not, whatever you do, borrow a pen or move any of this teacher's papers.

Advantages: Children know where they stand with this type of teacher. They will be well disciplined, although through fear rather than respect. Can achieve good results with able, well-motivated children.

Disadvantages: Quiet children are often too scared to answer questions and there is little group work. Weaker children may exhibit bad behaviour as an excuse to escape from the classroom. Difficult students can become confrontational.

Marks /10   Educational value = 6
Development of creativity and imagination = 1
Quality of discipline = 7
Equality of opportunity = 1
Scale of student appreciation = 2

Total score /50   **17**

'The students are my mates' teacher

Dress code: Dresses in a casual style, often wearing trendy labels. Tries to dress like the students to get 'in' with them. Not keen on school uniform; tends to overlook minor infringements of the uniform rules.

Favourite catchphrases: Aims to emulate the students, *'Check it out'* is a favourite. If a fight starts between students, uses *'C'mon, let's be reasonable about this dudes.'*

Discipline code: Bases the discipline code on the theory that, if you let the students do what they want, they are likely to work harder. Feels comfortable with lots of noise and activity.

Favourite method of discipline: Believes that: *'The students will discipline themselves if they feel sufficiently motivated and any misdemeanours are an expression of the students' frustration at an outmoded schooling system, which denies young people a sense of identity and seeks to destroy their natural creativity.'*

Teaching style: Lots of exploration and issues-based work, usually in groups. Avoids traditional 'chalk and talk' methods.

Marking strategy: Only gives positive comments and feels that using red ink demotivates the students. Strongly against the concept of a right or wrong answer.

Bad habits: Talking while the class are chatting; using too much jargon when talking to other teachers; smoking (sometimes *with* the students).

Classroom layout: Desks usually set out in groups, but sometimes likes to get rid of the furniture altogether and have an impromptu drama session.

State of teacher's desk: Neat desk, because all the papers are in one pile. At the bottom of the pile is an urgent form that was due in three weeks ago.

Advantages: Students like this teacher, partly because they feel relaxed, but also because they can get away with murder. This style encourages creativity and individuality.

Disadvantages: Chaos probably reigns. A noisy classroom atmosphere can be troubling for students who prefer to concentrate on their work.

Marks /10   Educational value = 7
Development of creativity and imagination = 9
Quality of discipline = 3
Equality of opportunity = 7
Scale of student appreciation = 7

Total score /50   **33**

The ultra-efficient teacher

Dress code: Always dresses smartly: if male, wears a suit and tie, if female, wears a smart jacket with a skirt. Imposes the school uniform rules consistently.

Favourite catchphrase: 'I'd like you all to face the front, make eye contact and listen carefully, thanks.'

Discipline code: Has a strong sense of discipline, but is not necessarily seen as strict by the children. Believes that everyone has an equal right to a good education and will impose the discipline necessary to achieve this.

Favourite method of discipline: Applies the school behaviour policy to the letter. Will contact the home if a child is consistently misbehaving.

Teaching style: Clear and well-organised lessons with a good balance between teacher and student input.

Marking strategy: Combines written comments with close marking of errors. Willing to spend hours on marking.

Bad habits: Cosies up to senior management because of an ambition to get quick promotion. Reports beautifully presented and handed in ahead of time.

Classroom layout: Desks set out in rows, facing the teacher, but will be moved for group work and returned immaculately to the previous position.

State of teacher's desk: Spotless, with lesson plans for each day carefully laid out in advance. Photocopied resources for the next three weeks are ready for use.

Advantages: Children know where they stand and respond well to the consistent standards. Work is neatly presented and children are given equal opportunities.

Disadvantages: Irritating and depressing to mere mortals, as we know we will never be this efficient.

Marks /10   Educational value = 9
                Development of creativity and imagination = 7
                Quality of discipline = 9
                Equality of opportunity = 9
                Scale of student appreciation = 7

                Total score /50   **41**

The joker

Dress code: Wears fairly casual, 'fun' clothes, brightly coloured ties and t-shirts with amusing captions. Couldn't care less about school uniform.

Favourite catchphrases: Starts every lesson by saying: *'Do you want to hear a joke?'* The joke will invariably be rude.

Discipline code: Feels that if the students find the lessons funny, they will behave themselves. Surprisingly, this often works.

Favourite method of discipline: Disciplines classes by making fun of any student who misbehaves. Joke punishments include the child standing in the corner, on one leg, with hands on head.

Teaching style: Uses personal anecdotes to illustrate a subject. For instance, geography work on polluted rivers may consist of a story about the time the joker and his or her mates got drunk and threw a shopping trolley into the local river. Likes to jump up on desks to add variety.

Marking strategy: Students' books full of jokey comments – the joker is happy for the students to respond to these in a similar vein.

Bad habits: See 'favourite catchphrases' (telling bad jokes) and 'dress code' (wearing bad ties). Favours strange haircuts.

Classroom layout: Desks set out in rows, facing front. This is not because of any particular educational philosophy, but so that all the students can hear the jokes and admire the accompanying demonstrations.

State of teacher's desk: Desk looks like a tornado has recently passed by. Has a drawer full of handy practical jokes to play on teachers and students.

Advantages: Students respond well – a lot of school can be boring, so it's good for them to have a laugh. Often have a surprising amount of respect for the joker.

Disadvantages: Not a lot of teaching goes on because so much time is spent telling jokes. The quiet students sit quietly while the louder ones get most of the attention.

Marks /10   Educational value = 6
Development of creativity and imagination = 9
Quality of discipline = 7
Equality of opportunity = 6
Scale of student appreciation = 9

Total score /50   **37**

The chaos theory teacher

Dress code: Looks as if the outfit was thrown together in a force ten hurricane in about ten seconds that morning. Hair appears slept on and has not seen a comb in recent history.

Favourite catchphrases: Usually spotted wandering around the staffroom asking, *'Has anybody got a red pen I can borrow?'* As exam time draws near, this will change to. *'I'm sure I had that set of really important GCSE exam papers a minute ago... now where did I put them?'*

Discipline code: What discipline code? Chaos rules and the children must sink or swim. Some students at the back of the room on the floor smoking cigarettes.

Favourite method of discipline: Believes that having a chat to the offenders to try and discover what makes them tick will work miracles.

Teaching style: Practises 'discovery learning' – translates as *'the kids do what they like and if I'm lucky a little bit of learning takes place'*. Highly intelligent but has trouble putting information across.

Marking strategy: Straightforward and works every time: lose the books before you have to mark them.

Bad habits: Absent-mindedly picking nose or scratching bottom. See also 'marking strategy' (losing books) and 'dress code' (incredibly messy).

Classroom layout: Desks set out in rows, to impose a bit of order on the class. By the end of the day/lesson rows are disbanded, by the students, rather than the teacher, so that friends can sit together.

State of teacher's desk: Looks like the proverbial bomb has hit it. Somewhere beneath the debris are those vital exam papers and lost exercise books.

Advantages: A true expert on many subjects and students respond well to this. Teaching style can lead to some very creative thinking.

Disadvantages: Bright kids may do well, the less able get lost in the whirlwind.

Marks /10   Educational value = 6
Development of creativity and imagination = 8
Quality of discipline = 2
Equality of opportunity = 4
Scale of student appreciation = 7

Total score /50   28

The earth mother or father

Dress code: If female, wears a long corduroy pinafore dress, flat shoes and hair tied back in a bun. If male, spot by the 'Jesus' sandals (worn, in impeccable style, with socks) and the long beard.

Favourite catchphrases: 'Now then, children, let's all settle down and do some work, shall we?' said as the class start to riot. Students are called 'children' up to school leaving age.

Discipline code: Tries to encourage self-discipline in the children; feels it is wrong for teachers to be disciplinarian. Asks quietly for silence and is ignored.

Favourite method of discipline: Believes in talking to the children about why they did what they did and why they shouldn't do it again.

Teaching style: Soft and gently spoken. Lessons consist of talking to the class for a while then asking them to explore a topic. Rarely raises voice, except when panic sets in as the class is rioting and the head is coming down the corridor.

Marking strategy: Only positive comments, no red pen or crosses allowed.

Bad habits: Talking while the children are talking; not washing hair frequently enough; wearing socks with sandals.

Classroom layout: Desks grouped, so that the children can 'share their ideas'. Lots of environmentally-friendly posters on the walls.

State of teacher's desk: Neat desk, with lots of little personal items, such as a cuddly toy, a photo of the family and a memento from Glastonbury 1976.

Advantages: Beneficial for quiet and weak children, as they receive lots of personal attention and a gentle, caring approach.

Disadvantages: Poor classroom control; lessons do not stretch the more able; those with behavioural difficulties may take advantage.

Marks /10   Educational value = 6
Development of creativity and imagination = 8
Quality of discipline = 5
Equality of opportunity – 7
Scale of student appreciation = 7

Total score /50   **33**

Working with support staff

When I first began teaching, there was rarely more than one adult in the room. These days, many teachers now have support staff working alongside them in the classroom. The help and expertise that they offer can be a very valuable asset in your NQT year and beyond. However, there are also issues to do with managing support staff, and making the best of them. You might work with classroom assistants, special needs workers, learning support assistants, behaviour support staff, and so on. To get the best out of your team use the following dos and don'ts.

Do

✓ Talk together frequently, negotiating the kind of role support staff wish to play.

✓ Draw on any prior experience of your support staff, for instance, with a particular class or child.

✓ Explore the kind of expertise that your support staff can offer, perhaps in a specific curriculum area or with displays.

✓ Encourage your assistant to give his or her own ideas about how best to deliver lesson activities and manage the classroom.

✓ Involve support staff when you are talking to the class, using inclusive language such as 'we' and 'us'. Let the children see you as a team.

Don't

✗ Allow the students to behave differently for support staff than they do for you. Maintain the same expectations and boundaries for you and any other staff.

✗ Always dictate what support staff must do. Ask them whether they would like to be involved in lesson planning or in differentiating tasks.

✗ Automatically send support staff off to work with small groups elsewhere.

✗ Dump all the difficult or dull jobs on your assistant – don't view him or her as someone who is there to remove challenging children from the class.

✗ Forget to use support staff to extend the most able, as well as to support those with additional learning needs.

Dealing with senior management

In your first year you will probably have very little reason to deal directly with members of the senior management team. However, if you have any problems you should usually turn to one of the following people:

- Your induction tutor.
- Your line manager.
- In a secondary school, your head of department.
- For issues with a tutor group, a head of year or other pastoral manager.

If you choose to apply for promotion, you will have increasing contact with senior managers. It is useful to have these staff on your side, as they can assist you if you have any major problems or if you need approval, for instance for a trip or for time off. Remember that members of the senior management of a school are 'on duty' at all times, so bear this in mind when you are dealing with them. Be careful what you say – what you see as a joke might be taken in the wrong way. I'm not suggesting that you need to crawl to senior staff, but don't forget who decides on the promotions in a school.

The best senior managers are those who:

✓ Still have a sense of the day to day realities of the classroom.

✓ Talk to *all* their staff, staying in daily contact and taking staff ideas on board where possible.

✓ Encourage a consistent approach amongst staff, where team work is a priority.

✓ Find ways to make a full time teaching post less stressful for their teachers.

✓ Minimise inessential paperwork, policies and meetings.

✓ Follow through with aspects such as behaviour management, taking the side of the staff wherever appropriate.

The worst senior managers are those who:

✗ Became managers because they couldn't 'hack it' in the classroom.

✗ Have forgotten completely about how hard and stressful the classroom can be.

✗ Have a fabulous but unrealistic 'vision' for their school, which they expect you to put into practice.

✗ Impose ideas, policies, etc. from above, rather than in consultation with teachers.

✗ Add unnecessary form filling and meetings to your workload.

Of course, you will form your own opinion of the senior managers at your school.

Chapter 10
Parents

What is this chapter about?

Your children's parents and carers play a crucial part in the success of your work with the children. You will quickly learn that those students who come from a supportive, caring home are far more likely to do well at school. In this chapter you will find ideas about developing your relationship with parents, thoughts about coping with parent consultation meetings, and also an examination of some of the different types of parents you might meet.

I use the term 'parents' throughout this chapter to describe whoever takes care of the child outside of school. There are of course many different types of family unit and a wide range of people who might be responsible for caring for your students. The term 'parents' is used to include all of these: from single parent families, to guardians such as foster parents, grandparents, brothers and sisters, looked after children, and so on.

Developing the teacher-parent relationship

Using the analogy between a school and a business, the parents of a student are the clients of the business. Of course, unless you are working at a private school, the parents are not paying directly for your 'services', but they are still doing so indirectly, through taxation. All parents are entitled to know (and many will demand) that the service offered by your school, and by you individually as a teacher, matches their expectations. As in any business, it is important to develop a good relationship with your clients. This is especially important in education because the parents can back up the work that you do in school with their child in the home. To develop your relationship with parents, remember to:

- *Explain how they can support you:* Many parents would like to support the work done by teachers, but are unsure how. Explain to them how they can help – reading with their child, helping them learn spellings, ensuring homework is completed, supporting you in behaviour management issues, etc.

- *Use parents as a source of information:* Ask your children to bring in details of a family tree for a history project or statistics about the size of their family for maths work. Students could record an interview with their parents for a project about schools through history.

- *Invite them into your classroom/school:* Some parents are willing to come into the classroom to assist the teacher, for instance to listen to readers. Other parents are happy to help with school events, for instance sewing costumes for your school production.

- *Get involved with your PTA:* Schools have a parent teacher group, the Parent-Teacher Association (PTA). The PTA strengthens the links between home and school and raises funds for the school. You might also request some funds from the PTA or school fundraising group for a project in your own class.

Communicating with parents

It is vital to keep the channels of communication open. This is typically much easier in the primary school, where you have only one set of parents to deal with, and there are more opportunities for informal contact. In the secondary school, you will need to make a concerted effort to communicate with parents. There are many ways to communicate with parents, including:

- Informal chats at drop off or pick up time.
- Formalised reports.
- Parents' consultation meetings.
- Via student diaries.
- Through a school or termly class newsletter.
- A class blog, updated weekly.
- The school website.
- Phone calls home.
- Letters home.

The parents' consultation meeting

One of the scariest experiences in your induction year will be your first ever parents' meeting. This might take place in the evening or, as is increasingly the case, during a special day set aside for teachers to meet with parents. As a trainee, although you may have come into contact with parents or carers, you will not have had to face them in such a formalised setting. Here are some dos and don'ts to help you prepare for and survive this nerve-racking occasion. Remember that after a few of these you will wonder what you were ever scared about.

Preparation
Do:

✓ Aim to bunch appointments together if you only have a few parents to see.

✓ Talk naturally and informally to the parents about your impressions of their child.

✓ Have a few points noted down if there are any specific concerns.

✓ Aim to have a break between school and the meetings, if they take place in the evening.

✓ Bring some fresh clothes so you can get changed and feel business-like.

✓ Have something to eat and drink before you begin, and keep a bottle of water on the table.

Don't:

✗ Make copious amounts of notes before the parents' evening – you are unlikely to refer to them.

✗ Face parents in a tired, stressed or harried state – have a quiet last lesson if the meetings are in the evening.

✗ Worry too much about the accuracy of appointment times – inevitably some appointments will run over, some parents will turn up late and some other teachers will talk for longer than they should.

✗ Insist on seeing the parents of every child if you teach a large number of students (e.g. you teach a secondary subject such as art, drama or PE). Focus on those you most need to talk with.

At the meeting

Do:

✓ Aim to put parents at their ease. When they arrive, stand up, shake hands and identify which child they 'belong to'.

✓ If the student is with the parents, as a starter question, ask *'How do you think you've been getting on?'*

✓ Have the child's books, or a piece of work, ready to show the parents (you might have these available for parents to read while they wait).

✓ Keep what you say concise and to the point – comment on the child's work to date and set some targets for the future.

✓ Bring the discussion to a close by saying 'Do you have any questions?'

Don't:

✗ Forget that most parents will be as or even more nervous than you are.

✗ Talk too fast, or use overly technical or fancy terminology.

✗ Waffle on endlessly about the child – stick to the point or you will end up exhausted.

✗ Worry if parents have a query you can't answer. Make a note and say that you will talk to a senior member of staff.

Problems/problem parents

Although it is unusual, you may find yourself in a situation where parents become confrontational, perhaps criticising the way you teach or the type of work you are setting. As an inexperienced teacher, this can be difficult to handle. If this does happen, try to remain calm and rational, using the techniques discussed in Chapter 3 to defuse the situation. You might suggest a meeting with a senior teacher at another time. In this way the parents can discuss their concerns in a private setting and you will have the support of a more experienced colleague.

Missing?

Inevitably, some parents will not turn up, either because they were busy, because they did not want to come or because the student did not tell them that there was a parents' evening. It is often the case that the parents you most want or need to talk to do not arrive. Aim to check up on any students you are worried about. Your school may have a system where they do this for you, but if you have strong concerns make a phone call home yourself (having told the appropriate pastoral manager first).

Types of parent

You will come across a variety of parents in your teaching career: the majority being genuinely supportive people who want to help you succeed in teaching their child. A minority of parents will be less helpful and some may prove very difficult to deal with. Always stay calm, polite and professional when you are speaking to parents, no matter how much they antagonise you. A good way to avoid confrontation is to use some of the tactics you would employ with a difficult student.

I would like to offer you some ideas about how to deal with some different types of parents, including my 'top tips'. The way you handle parents will vary according to the situation you find yourself in and also the policies of your school or department. The best advice is to concentrate on doing your job as well as you can, and not to worry too much if you encounter the occasional conflict.

Supportive parents

Supportive parents are a delight to work with: they believe that you know your job, but they are there to back you up should you ever need it. They encourage their children to do the best they can and to take the work and homework you set seriously.

Top Tip: Involve this type of parent as much as you can with the school, for instance asking them to visit your class to give a talk or to help individual students.

Overambitious parents

It is difficult to deal with this type of parent. They want the best for their children, but unfortunately their ambitions sometimes outstrip what the children are capable of, or what the students want for themselves. These parents can make life difficult for the teacher, asking why you have set particular work and suggesting that you don't know how to do your job.

Top Tip: The best policy with this type of parent is to humour them, but not to alter what you have decided to teach because of them.

Overprotective parents

Some parents worry a great deal about how their children are settling into school, and because of this have a negative impact on the child's confidence. The overprotective parent might be a useful candidate for a classroom volunteer – then the parent can see how the child is coping, and can help some of the children who need additional assistance.

Top Tip: Answer the parents' concerns, particularly if you are the child's tutor or primary class teacher. Reassure them that you will look out for their child and promise to keep them informed.

Parents who abdicate responsibility

This type of parent believes that the child is the school's problem, and that you should deal with any difficulties that come up. They believe that their responsibility ends when the child leaves home each morning.

Top Tip: Be aware that the child may see school in a negative light and will probably need lots of praise and encouragement.

Potentially abusive parents

If you suspect that a child is being abused, notify your child protection officer (CPO) and the appropriate pastoral or senior manager immediately. They may be aware of the situation, but you would not be doing your job (and you would be failing the child) if you did not make your concerns known. It is not your responsibility to deal with such serious problems and you do not have the specialist knowledge required to do so.

Top Tip: If you're ever unsure, pass your concerns on, in writing, straight away.

Dealing with complaints

From time to time, parents will complain, either about what or how you are teaching. You will know whether these complaints are justified, and for the most part they will not be. Unfortunately they really are just part of the job. Stick to your guns – if the work you have set is in line with departmental or school policies, if the sanctions you have given are fair and the student has earned them, then you are acting professionally. Be confident in yourself: even though you have only just started teaching, you have undertaken the appropriate training for your role.

If a parent complains directly to you, talk to an experienced member of staff before responding. Your induction tutor, pastoral manager or head of department will have experience in dealing with parents and can help you decide what to do. Explain the situation as clearly as you can, stating exactly what you have done and why. Your colleagues should be more than willing to back you up. If the parent complains indirectly, perhaps to your head of department or line manager, find out exactly what they said and again make your position clear. Talk with your union rep as appropriate, but try not worry too much. These complaints really are unavoidable, even for the best and most experienced teachers in a school.

PART V

Just Part of the Job

Chapter 11
Meetings and extra-curricular activities

What is this chapter about?

After a long day at school, you will find at least some of your evenings taken up with meetings and probably with extra-curricular activities as well. Depending on how well they are run, meetings can feel like a very valuable part of your job, or a complete waste of time. The extra-curricular work you do after school will generally offer a much more positive experience. Many of the staff who run these activities do so not because it is a statutory requirement, but because they genuinely enjoy the experience. In this chapter you can find some ideas about meetings, as well as about the plus and minus sides of involvement in extra-curricular activities.

Different kinds of meetings

Generally speaking there are two kinds of staff meeting: the regular briefing-type meeting which is fairly short and deals with the day-to-day practicalities of running a school; and the formalised meeting of all the staff that takes place perhaps once a term. The main features of each type of meeting differ quite substantially. On the next page is a quick guide to each type.

The staff briefing

- Usually held about once a day or once/twice a week.
- Useful for communicating information between all the staff within a school.
- Used for passing on details about individual students, or for informing staff about upcoming events.
- Good for communicating information that you need everyone to know right away.
- Far less formal than a full staff meeting.
- Usually opened by the head/deputy head giving information.
- After this, the floor is opened to the staff, who raise a hand if they wish to contribute.

The formal staff meeting

- Part of your 'directed time' – the statutory hours that you must work.
- Usually timetabled well in advance on a school calendar.
- Normally take place after school, or on an INSET day, in the staffroom or the school hall.
- Usually much longer than a staff briefing – may go on for two hours or more.
- An agenda will be published and sent out perhaps a week ahead of the meeting.
- Most of the speaking is usually done by the head or a deputy.
- Covers whole-school issues such as rewriting policies, action and development plans, and so on.

The department/subject/co-ordinators meeting

- Subject-specific meetings usually take place about once a month.
- Sometimes before/after school, sometimes during a lunch break or free period.
- A valuable time for updates on the latest curriculum issues, training, materials, etc.
- You might also discuss moderation, SATs, exam boards, schemes of work.
- These meetings are also used for disseminating information about training that staff have attended.
- An informal atmosphere, often quite a fun and valuable experience (or as fun as meetings can be!).

The meetings trap

As well as these 'statutory' meetings, there will be many other meetings going on after school. Your presence will not be required at most of these, as attendance is often limited to staff in positions of responsibility. However, there could also be other working parties that meet perhaps once per half-term.

At the start of the year, each department or key stage may be asked to put forward staff to sit on these working parties. As with extra-curricular activities, it can be valuable to be able to say you were on a working party when you apply for other jobs, as it shows you are willing to get involved in every aspect of the running of a school. Similarly, you may value the chance to meet staff from other departments or areas of the school, and you may have some excellent ideas or a specialism of your own that you would like to develop.

However, do not feel pressurised into joining these groups unless you are sure you have the time. No one will mind if an inexperienced teacher does not volunteer to help out, but you could find that others take advantage because you are fresh, uncynical and enthusiastic to offer your services. If you can guarantee that you will only have to attend a couple of meetings a term, and make no other time-consuming contributions, then it may be worth your while volunteering. However, beware of the 'meetings trap' whereby you end up doing lots of additional paperwork, writing plans, disseminating information to your department, and so on. If you are involved with a lot of extra curricular activities, for instance if you teach sport, drama or music, you will have a very good get-out clause.

Extra-curricular activities

People often associate extra-curricular activities with teachers who are specialists in particular subjects, for instance drama teachers (the school play), music teachers (the school choir and orchestra) and PE teachers (football, netball teams, and so on). However, there is no reason why this should be so and it is worth getting involved with this aspect of the school if you possibly can, even if you do not see yourself as a specialist.

In my experience, the advantages of taking part in extra-curricular activities far outweigh the disadvantages. In independent schools, or if you are a teacher of a subject such as PE, there may be an element of compulsion for you to participate. Even if this is not the case, it is still worth getting involved. Do be careful though not to take on too much while you are an NQT. Ask your mentor if you're not sure.

The advantages

✓ You get to know the students, meeting children who you don't currently teach (but may do in the future).

✓ The atmosphere is more relaxed, so you can show a different side of yourself to the children.

✓ You also see a different side to students, for instance seeing that 'difficult' child work really well within a sports team.

✓ The relationship you build can have significant benefits for your work in lessons with the children.

✓ Your colleagues will really appreciate that extra set of hands, and will probably find a way to help you out in turn in the future.

✓ Taking part in extra-curricular activities is very useful indeed for your CV.

✓ You will get to develop new skills and experiences, perhaps ones that you might not get the chance to develop otherwise.

✓ You work as part of a team, and perhaps with staff from subject areas other than your own.

✓ It can be very personally satisfying, and a great deal of fun!

The disadvantages

✗ It can be a significant time commitment, and you'll need to decide whether you can afford to take this time away from planning and other vital jobs.

✗ If you have a family of your own, it may not be possible to combine the two without your family losing out.

✗ Once you start getting involved after school, the activities have a tendency to escalate as people realise you are willing to get involved and pile on the responsibility.

✗ Your induction tutor and line manager might feel that this is not the most appropriate use of your time.

Some tips on trips

One of the most memorable school experiences for many children is the chance to go on a trip. Some might not otherwise have this opportunity, perhaps because of financial considerations. Trips can seem like a great adventure for students because they get out of school and see a little of the real world. Of course, trips also have a very valid educational justification. For the teacher, too, a trip is the chance to get out of school for a day or more and get to know the students better in a different environment.

If you are approached to take part in a trip, for instance a visit to a museum, an art gallery or the theatre, say 'yes' immediately. There is no reason why a relatively inexperienced teacher should not organise a trip. If you are interested in doing this, or in taking part in a trip that someone else has arranged, read the tips on the next page carefully.

Follow the school policy to the letter

First and foremost I would caution you to ensure that your school or LEA trips' policy is followed to the letter. Work together with a more experienced colleague who is willing to support and assist you. There are legal obligations involved with taking students out of school and it is very important that you are aware of these. You are *in loco parentis* – in the role of a parent – and if there are any problems you are legally responsible. You will also need to complete paperwork such as risk assessments and so on.

Have plenty of supervision

Find out the specific requirements for your age range. If you are taking a large group try to find a range of teachers from different subject areas or age groups to accompany you.

Be aware of all the administrative jobs

Before you go you will need to get letters sent home, asking for permission, and also for a voluntary contribution towards the costs. You will have to ensure that return slips and money are collected, so leave sufficient time before the trip for admin staff to do this. Schools should have a budget set aside to help students who cannot afford the cost of trips so check how this works before you start.

Organise transport carefully

If the trip is by coach, ask other staff about advice on a company to use. If the trip is taking place outside of normal school hours, arrange a meeting-place for your students. At the end of the trip this could be where you will drop them off with parents. Supervise them until they have all been collected.

Keep an eye on behaviour

The students will probably get excited during the trip: it is your duty to calm them down and ensure that they behave themselves in the appropriate way.

Put it on your CV

This is an excellent experience to have on your CV when you apply for jobs. It shows initiative and also, as with any extra-curricular activity, a willingness to become involved with all aspects of school life. If you do not have the opportunity or confidence to organise your own trip, aim to get invited on a trip organised by other members of staff.

Chapter 12
Induction, appraisal and inspection

What is this chapter about?

Your teaching practices will have given you a good idea of what life as a teacher is really like, but it is only during your first year in the profession that you actually *become* a teacher. Part of the whole process of becoming a qualified teacher is passing your NQT year. The actual arrangements for induction or probation vary in different areas of the country, but overall the process has a number of similarities. In this chapter you can find out all about what to expect during your NQT year, including tips on how to do your best during appraisals. In addition, you'll find some advice and ideas about inspection.

Try not to focus too much on 'passing induction/inspection' or on 'passing your NQT year'. The key to success is to concentrate on what really matters, i.e. how well the children are learning and how you are developing your skills in the classroom to help them do this. If you do the job to the best of your ability, the probability is that you will succeed – the majority of NQTs do.

Induction: what to expect

The government publishes guidelines which specify what should happen during your induction year. How well these are followed will vary from school to school. If you are lucky, your induction tutor or mentor will be experienced, effective and, perhaps most importantly, available when you need to talk. Unfortunately, this isn't always the case.

It can be difficult as an NQT to complain if the induction guidelines are not being followed – make sure you know about your entitlements and what to do if they are not being met. Remember that it is you who will pass or fail, and this could depend on the kind of support your school offers. Make it a priority to read up on the relevant guidance. Turn to your LEA or union for support if things are not going well.

During induction you can expect to receive the following:

✓ Help and support from experienced teachers.

✓ An induction tutor will support and observe you.

✓ Non-contact time to help you cope with and adapt to the workload.

✓ Observations of your lessons.

✓ Assessments of your teaching, both formal and informal.

✓ Setting of targets and objectives on which you can work.

✓ Professional development, for instance additional training.

At the same time, you should not:

✗ Be given especially challenging classes to deal with.

✗ Have to teach for more than 90% of a normal timetable.

✗ Be given additional responsibilities outside of your classroom role.

✗ Have 'unreasonable demands' made of you.

✗ Be asked to teach outside of the age range and subjects for which you have been employed.

You can find lots of useful internet links about induction in Appendix Two.

The role of the induction mentor

Your induction tutor or mentor plays a vital role when you start teaching: he or she is the person you turn to if you have any questions or problems. Your tutor is also responsible for watching some of your lessons to evaluate your progress. The induction tutor should check that you are not taking on too much on top of your classroom role. If you are lucky enough to have a good and supportive tutor, this will make your NQT year much easier.

You should have regular meetings with your tutor, at which you set targets, assess your progress, and deal with any concerns that you may have. A little way into your first term, you should discuss your first formal evaluation. Hopefully, your tutor will allow you to choose a particular subject or class for this observation. It is not necessarily beneficial to choose an 'easy' lesson: it may be better to show your tutor and yourself how you deal with difficult or challenging subjects or students.

Getting the most from your induction mentor

As a new teacher, you may feel at a disadvantage in the relationship between you and your mentor, who will have more experience than you. Remember, though, that your tutor will probably have volunteered for the role and how well you do will reflect on him or her. The dos and don'ts below will help you in getting the most from your induction tutor, and in developing a good relationship.

Do:

- ✓ Be specific about the support that you want.
- ✓ Be proactive – ask for time to chat if it is not offered and you need it.
- ✓ Set a time to meet, rather than always trying to catch your mentor when he/she is passing.

✓ Let your mentor know when you take on additional responsibilities, both to show your enthusiasm, and also to gain advice on balancing your workload.

✓ Ask your mentor to go through the specifics of the induction process with you.

✓ Look out for good quality training opportunities, particularly those where both you and your mentor can attend.

Don't:

✗ Hassle your tutor at break or between lessons, when he or she has other things to do.

✗ Pretend everything is fine if it isn't – be honest when you're having problems.

✗ Moan about your mentor to other colleagues behind his/her back, even if you're not getting on very well – it's very unprofessional.

Successful appraisals

Experienced teachers are required to undergo regular appraisals, evaluations or observations – sometimes called 'performance management'. This type of testing should be viewed as an important and useful part of your job, because it can help you become a better teacher. Appraisers take different approaches when they evaluate a class: some like to get involved, moving around to question the students, to look at books (and check your marking) and to help anyone who needs it; others may simply sit in a corner at the back of the room and watch what goes on from there. You could ask your appraiser ahead of time whether he or she is willing to assist you in a particular part of the lesson. This would demonstrate initiative on your part and, if your appraiser happens to be a teacher in your subject area, he or she could be a valuable resource for you.

When you or your appraiser have chosen a lesson for evaluation, you should prepare carefully for this formalised review. You will, of course, have been observed many times during your training. Indeed, recent graduates are probably better prepared for this process than those who have been in teaching for a long time. You will have many things on your mind when you are being appraised, but it is important for you to show what a good classroom teacher you are. Use the diagram below to help you do just that.

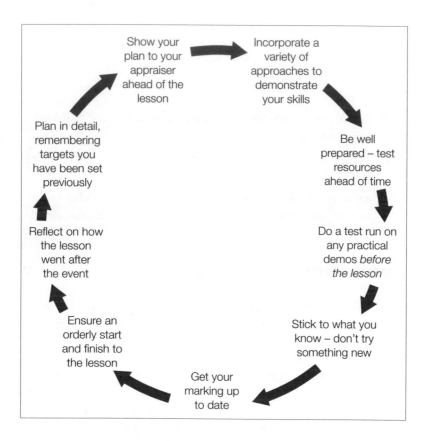

Show your plan to your appraiser ahead of the lesson

Incorporate a variety of approaches to demonstrate your skills

Plan in detail, remembering targets you have been set previously

Be well prepared – test resources ahead of time

Reflect on how the lesson went after the event

Do a test run on any practical demos *before the lesson*

Ensure an orderly start and finish to the lesson

Stick to what you know – don't try something new

Get your marking up to date

Feedback

After the appraisal, get the feedback you are entitled to, as soon as possible. Teachers are busy people, but there is no point in being appraised if you do not find out what you did right or wrong and how you might improve. Your feedback sessions should include:

- Verbal feedback about what went well and what didn't.

- A detailed written evaluation for formal assessments.
- Positive feedback about what's going well.
- Constructive criticisms about how you can improve.
- A chance to state your own opinions or to ask questions.
- Targets and objectives to work towards for your next appraisal.

You should receive a copy of your formal written evaluations and the school will put another copy on your personnel file. Your appraiser will ask you to read the evaluation and to sign it to show that you have had the opportunity to discuss it.

Surviving inspection

How unlucky do you have to be for your school to receive an inspection when you have only just started teaching? Statistically, the chances must be quite slim, but it is by no means impossible. The longer you stay at any school, the more chance there is that the inspectors will pay a visit sooner or later. The 'failing' schools and 'failing' teachers rooted out by the inspectors receive a great deal of publicity; the successful and thriving schools seem to get very little.

Preparing for inspection

If you are at a school which is likely to do badly in its inspection, remember that as an inexperienced teacher you have very little responsibility. As long as you are doing your job in the classroom to the best of your ability, and consistently striving to improve your teaching, there is very little for you to worry about. As someone who has just come into the profession, all the latest developments will be fresh in your memory. You may also be more enthusiastic and have more energy than the teachers who have been in the job for a long time. As an NQT, your school should be supporting you in becoming a qualified teacher, which may not be happening if you're in a badly run school.

In the old days, when I began teaching, schools would receive warning of an inspection well in advance. This advance warning had its good and bad points: it gave the school plenty of time to prepare, to get documentation in place, to help the weaker teachers improve (and perhaps exclude some of the more difficult students). However, it also led to a climate of expectation in which rumours abounded about the horrors of inspection. These days there is a much shorter lead in time before the inspectors arrive, although schools will still have some sense of when an inspection is likely to occur.

The myths

The myths about inspection seem to multiply and take on a life of their own. The senior managers at your school will, of course, be under a lot of stress during an inspection. They may warn you that everything you say will be taken down and used in evidence against the school; that the inspectors will be particularly concerned with your subject or age range; that every lesson plan and department handbook will be closely scrutinised.

It is possible that you will be asked to use a particular format to prepare your lesson plans and your school may work itself into a frenzy, checking that handbooks and schemes of work are in place. You may be warned that, if the inspectors come to see you and don't like what they see, they will keep returning again and again to your class. The myth might circulate that you are sacked on the spot if you 'fail' (i.e. if you receive a bad score for a particular lesson).

The reality

In reality, it is likely that your lessons will be observed no more than a few times during an inspection, if at all. There are often relatively few inspectors to go around and some inspectors will cover more than one subject or age range. In an inspection at my first school, when we reached Thursday of the inspection week and I still had not been 'seen', my head of department had to *request* that someone observed one of my lessons so that the inspectors could see the practice going on in our department. This situation may, of course, vary in a smaller school or at primary level. However, even if you are 'seen' by the inspectors on several occasions, this does not mean that they have found anything wrong with your teaching.

When an inspector arrives in your lesson he or she might ask for a copy of the lesson plan, so have this easily to hand. Even if you are not asked, hand over the lesson plan anyway. After all, you have spent all that time preparing for your moment of glory and you should show the inspectors exactly how good you are. Irritatingly, this means that you will have to have detailed plans ready for every lesson that you are due to teach while the inspectors are in the building. However, the amount of information required is not great. It is fairly unlikely that the inspector, with a full timetable of classes to watch, will be able to stay for the entire length of the lesson. It is of course likely that they will leave just as the best bit of your lesson begins.

Inspection and the NQT

As a new teacher you will probably have no curriculum responsibility and will only be responsible for ensuring that you teach your own class or classes properly. This means that if a secondary school department is disorganised, it will not be you that comes under fire. The head of your department has responsibility for ensuring that all documentation is correct and in place: schemes of work, handbooks, and so on. If an inspector comes to watch your lessons, he or she will know that you are an NQT and should take this into account. Above all, don't panic – do the job to the best of your ability, and have confidence in your teaching.

PART VI

Onwards and Upwards

Chapter 13
Professional development and promotion

What is this chapter about?

Towards the end of your first year, you may find yourself considering your future in the profession. You will certainly be encouraged to consider how you might develop yourself as a professional, whether this is by applying for promotion or by taking courses to learn new skills and further your teaching qualifications. In this chapter I deal with the issues of professional development and promotion. Even if you decide not to step onto the promotions ladder at this stage, it is still worth considering how you might wish to move onwards and upwards within your current school, or elsewhere, in the future.

Professional development

Your training as a teacher does not end once you qualify and your school should give you the opportunity for further development. There are various different forms of professional development, including:

- INSET (in-service training), which will usually take place in school at the start or end of term, when the students are not there.
- Twilight sessions (training held after the school day has finished).

- Public training courses run by external organisations (sometimes private companies, or organisations such as local football clubs).

- LEA training courses, often run at a reduced price, or for free.

- Postgraduate qualifications such as an MA, perhaps part time or in the evenings, maybe even funded by your school.

These are all part of your entitlement to EPD (early professional development) and CPD (continuing professional development). Take as many training opportunities as you can, because training has many benefits:

- It gives you a chance to develop and update your knowledge about teaching – things move very fast indeed in the world of education.

- The chance for a break – a day out of school may be just what you need, particularly in the second term.

- The chance to network, to talk with colleagues and NQTs from other schools.

- It's great to put on your CV.

It's a great idea to keep a little notebook in which you write down all the courses you've been on, etc. for future reference.

Aiming for promotion?

At some point in your teaching career, you will want to decide just how far you would like to advance within the profession. The time towards the end of your NQT year is a good time to consider this. You will still hopefully be enthusiastic about the profession, and you will have the benefit of a year's experience of what the job is really like. Below are some thoughts about aiming for promotion.

Promotions rely on many different factors

Teaching promotions are not just about how good you are at your job. Being in the right place at the right time when a post becomes available is often a key element in gaining promotion. Being the right person to fit into the management structure is also important.

You may need to move school to find promotion

Because of the limited movement available within any one school, you may find that no promotion opportunities occur. Teachers have a tendency to stay in post, particularly in well run schools.

The nature of your job will change

As you get promoted, your teaching timetable should become a little lighter. Consider carefully whether you want to spend less time in the classroom and more on paperwork and managerial tasks. More senior staff tend to deal with all the things that go wrong.

There's nothing wrong with staying in the classroom

There is quite a lot of pressure in teaching to aim for promotion, but there is no compulsion to do so. Some teachers dedicate their careers to becoming the best teacher they can be: they find satisfaction in committing themselves to their students.

Promotion means better pay

One of the reasons teachers aim for promotion is financial: as a classroom teacher you will reach the ceiling of the standard pay scale after around seven years. The points that come with promotion will boost your salary, although never by a really substantial amount.

Different types of promotion are available

There are generally two types of promoted position: pastoral and curriculum. A pastoral role involves looking after the students' needs and welfare, while a curriculum role includes teaching and managing a specific subject or group of subjects. Which type would suit you best?

Types of promotion

The table on the following page shows some likely routes for promotion in a secondary school. In the primary school the options are a little more limited – here you might move into a subject co-ordinator's role before becoming a deputy or assistant head.

Pastoral	Curriculum
Deputy head of year/house	Key Stage 3/4 co-ordinator (often only English, maths and science)
Head of year/house	Deputy head of department
Deputy or assistant head teacher	Head of department
Headteacher	Head of faculty

You can of course move across from the top of the curriculum to the top of the pastoral route.

The advantages of promotion

When you are deciding whether or not to go for promotion, it is worth taking some time to consider the pros and cons. The advantages of taking a promoted post would include:

- ✓ An increase in salary.
- ✓ More responsibility.
- ✓ More chance to impact on the future success of your school.
- ✓ Increased job satisfaction and influence.
- ✓ Developing your own subject area.
- ✓ Easier relationships with students who see you as an 'authority figure'.

The disadvantages of promotion

You will also need to weigh up the negative aspects of a change in role before going for a more senior post. These disadvantages would include:

- ✗ A more stressful role, managing staff as well as students.
- ✗ A change to the informal relationships with your colleagues.
- ✗ Working outside your area of expertise, so you spend less time on the subjects you love.
- ✗ You'll generally be working more with the needy/difficult students (although some people may view as an advantage).
- ✗ Your 'persona' will have to change, so that you are 'in role' at all times, including outside of school.
- ✗ You'll have an additional workload and more responsibility – the buck will stop with you when things go wrong!

Chapter 14
Moving on

What is this chapter about?

Some teachers decide to stay at the same school for many years; others are keen to move on quickly. This might be because of a negative experience at a school, or because they are seeking promotion or a fresh challenge. If you get to the end of your NQT year and find yourself considering a move, think very carefully before going through with it. No matter how tough the school, life will always be a bit easier in your second year within the setting, because you know the children, the staff, the systems and the place. Perhaps you do need to make a fresh start in a new school, or perhaps you are thinking about leaving the profession. The information and ideas in this chapter will help you when you do decide to move on.

The right school?

Towards the end of your NQT year, you will have a fair idea about whether this is the right school for you. It is important to differentiate between the inevitable tiredness associated with the end of the year and the need to find a new school (or career). There is no point in going through the work of looking for another teaching job (you remember – the endless form filling and letters of application) if you are going to be moving from the proverbial frying pan into the fire.

Look around your local area to see if there are any schools that interest you, and perhaps drop in to visit some of them, particularly if there are jobs available. Remember, there is a lot more to choosing a school than considerations about how difficult the students are – the management will make a huge difference as well. Remember also that no school is perfect: decide whether the good points about your school outweigh the bad. Moving on after only one year is a big decision, especially as you will just be familiarising yourself with the way things work.

Think also about how long you want to stay in one place: in the teaching profession there is a strong temptation to stay at the same school for a long time – after a while it becomes easier not to move. You know the children, the staff, the systems; you may have gained promotion within your department or subject, but is it necessarily beneficial for you or for the school to stay on? To help you decide whether a move is a good idea, use the questions below to think about how well your school does:

Management

- Are the managers at your school approachable and flexible?
- Are they willing to support and develop the teachers?
- Do the managers respond to staff suggestions for change?
- Have they lost touch with what it means to be in a classroom?
- Do senior staff ever spend time in the classroom?
- Or do they hide in an office, handing down commands from above?
- How well do managers relate to the students?
- When there are behaviour issues, do you get the back up you need?
- How well have your managers supported you during your NQT year?
- Have they resolved any problems that you experienced?
- What kind of opportunities for personal development/promotion have you been given?

Staff

- Do the staff at your school relate well to each other?
- Are teachers and other staff supportive of each other's ideas?
- How much cynicism and laziness have you seen?
- Is this about disillusionment with the job or with the school?
- Do staff tend to talk about the school in a positive or negative way?
- Do the different years/departments/areas within your school work together or in isolation?
- How well do you get on with the staff at your school?
- Do you respect their professionalism, or have at least a few things in common?
- Do you have good relationships with the support staff and other people who work at the school?
- How busy is the staffroom at breaks and lunchtimes?
- Do the staff ever socialise together?

Support systems

- Who can you turn to if you have a problem?
- Is your line manager an effective support?
- If not, is there someone else who can help you?
- Do the staff in your school support each other both inside and outside the classroom?
- Who supports the students in your school when they have problems?
- Is this done properly, or are issues swept under the carpet?
- Who supports any teachers when they are facing problems?
- Is this done effectively?
- Are staff ever undermined or bullied?

Your year group/key stage/department team

- How well does your year group leader, key stage co-ordinator or head of department suit the role?
- Do all members of your team pull their weight equally?
- Are you getting the opportunities you need for professional development?
- If you are aiming for promotion, are the opportunities available?
- Would you like to work in a smaller/larger team?

The students

- Do the children at your school show respect for each other?
- Is respect shown to teachers and support staff?
- How do students treat their environment?
- Is there a good mix of students who all get along with each other?
- What kind of children do you enjoy teaching?
- Do you relish the challenge of handling difficult behaviour?
- Would you prefer an 'easier life' at a private/grammar school (although bear in mind an increased marking load and more parental pressure)?
- Do you find the students interesting to teach?
- What are links like between your school and the students' homes?
- What kind of a 'difference' do you want to make to your children?

The curriculum

- Is your school innovative in the way it approaches the curriculum?
- Are managers up to date with the latest thoughts, ideas and innovations?
- Do you see yourself as overly bound by government guidelines and strategies?

- How well is the curriculum organised?
- Does your subject or age range get the resources it deserves?
- In a secondary school, how are the subjects divided?
- Are there faculties where several subjects are grouped together, or do the departments remain very much divided?
- Are you able to take a creative, forward-thinking approach?

Administration, paperwork and meetings

- Does your school make every effort to keep time-wasting admin and paperwork to a minimum?
- Are reports seen as a vital and informative method of communicating with the home, or are they an ineffective use of your time?
- Are meetings run efficiently and a valuable part of school life?
- Do you get the chance to contribute to the future direction of your school?
- Or, is only a token gesture paid towards genuine consultation with all the staff?

Buildings and facilities

- Are the buildings and facilities of a good quality?
- Is the fabric of the school well maintained?
- Is there any graffiti – do the students care for their environment?
- What are the students' toilet facilities like (often a surprisingly strong indicator of how a school views its children)?
- Is the space you teach in adequate for you?
- Does your teaching space inspire and enthuse you?
- Does your environment make you feel negative and depressed?
- If you have any complaints about your environment are they taken seriously and dealt with quickly or not?

Promotion

- Are you going to be looking for promotion in the near future?
- Are you interested in a subject, pastoral or managerial route?
- What opportunities are available in your school?
- Do your managers see your professional development as important?
- How are they going about promoting this aspect of your role?

Extra-curricular activities

- Are there a variety of extra-curricular activities at your school?
- Are these activities well supported by staff and students?
- Do a variety of staff get involved, or is the job of running them left to the more enthusiastic teachers?
- Are parents keen to get involved with the day to day life of the school?
- Do parents help out with after school clubs?

References

When you apply for your next job the school will usually ask for two referees, probably your head teacher and your head of department or line manager. If you are efficient and get on well with these people, you should have no problem getting good references. There's a well known opinion in teaching that those teachers who are completely hopeless will also get a good reference, on the basis that this is the best way for the head teacher to get rid of them.

When asking for a reference, make sure that your managers have a list of all those 'extras' you have been involved with, such as after school activities or working parties. Remember to tell your referees that you have applied for a new job *before* they receive a request for references. It is only polite and it will improve the chances of your receiving a good reference. Make sure that your managers also have some information about the type of job you are applying for, so they can adapt their reference to suit.

Applying for jobs

As the year passes, you will take part in many different aspects of school life; make sure that you keep a note of all the 'little extras' that you contribute to your school. When you come to write the letter of application for your next job, it's a pain to realise that you cannot remember which working parties you were on, how many plays or concerts you helped with, and so on. Write *everything* down as you go along – you might use a little notebook specially for this purpose. Schools want to know that you are an enthusiastic teacher who gets involved with all aspects of the life of the school. Demonstrate in your letter of application how you have done this at your current school.

Even if you are not desperate to move, bear in mind that if you get an interview for a job it will be good experience (and will get you a day out of school). Going for an interview will also demonstrate to your managers that you are looking for further development in your career. If you are an asset to the teaching staff at your school, they may decide that they do not want to lose you, and consequently try to offer you some sort of internal promotion or development. Be realistic about the jobs that you apply for – there is not usually much point in applying for a job which is more than two or three salary points above your own.

Is teaching the job for you?

After training as a teacher, there is a temptation to remain in the profession, even if you are not sure that it is the right job for you. At the end of your first year you will have gained some experience and can make a more rational judgement about your choice of career. Remember that teaching becomes easier the more experienced you become – the first year or two is always hard, no matter how talented a teacher you are.

Think very carefully if you are having doubts about teaching, during your lovely, long summer holiday. Perhaps have a chat with an experienced member of staff who you can trust to be discreet. Remember also that you may just be in the wrong school or teaching the wrong type of students for you. If you came into teaching straight from school/university, it might be that you need to take a couple of years out. Doing office work might help you feel more positive about the profession. Similarly, perhaps a move to teach abroad for a while might be a good idea at some point in your career.

It's interesting to note that there is a high 'leakage' from the profession, with behaviour and workload being cited as two of the most common reasons for leaving teaching. The statistics vary, but some studies have shown that up to 60% of those who originally enter training will *no longer be working full time in the classroom* after five years.

The following lists give some of the plus and minus points of teaching as a profession and may be helpful to you in deciding whether it is or is not the career for you.

The rewards

✓ You are your own boss – to an extent you teach what you want.

✓ You are working with the subject that you enjoy, day after day.

✓ You are working with children, day after day.

✓ There is good job security and it is a relatively well paid career.

✓ The job is as creative as you want to make it.

✓ The job is as big as you want to make it.

✓ The job is *never* boring.

✓ You can make a real difference to your children.

✓ You can form lasting relationships with students and staff.

✓ If you are good, your children will always remember you.

✓ There is excellent variety from day to day.

✓ You can gain valuable experience of a variety of tasks and situations.

✓ The actual school day is very short.

✓ It is a good job to combine with having a family.

✓ The teachers' pension is a good perk.

✓ The holidays really are very good indeed – this is a *big* perk. (If you're not convinced about this, just ask any office worker on 20 days' annual leave.)

The negative aspects

✗ The job is physically and emotionally tiring.

✗ The job expands to meet the extent of your dedication.

✗ You will encounter difficult and even disturbed children (and parents).

✗ You may be put at risk of injury from these people.

✗ The nature of the job can lead to cynicism.

✗ The salary will never be brilliant and only rises fairly slowly.

✗ Your friends in most other professions will rapidly start earning more than you.

✗ There is a lack of genuine promotion prospects for many teachers.

✗ Ironically, experienced teachers become too expensive for some schools.

✗ You will often have to work late, in your own time, to do a good job.

✗ You may be too tired to appreciate those lovely long holidays.

Leaving

So, you've made the decision to leave your school/the profession, and now the moment has come. You've told your children and been faced with reactions from *'Great!'* to *'Please, Miss/Sir, don't leave'*. Leaving is a double-edged sword – on the one hand you will find out how your students really feel about you (hopefully good), on the other hand you will be leaving behind colleagues and children that you genuinely care about, having worked with them closely for a long time. You may also feel guilty about leaving some secondary level classes half-way through a GCSE course. Don't – if you use this as a reason not to leave, you will never get out of your first school.

On your last day you will hopefully receive lots of cards and presents. You may have to give a leaving speech, but remember one thing before you list all the grievances you have about the school or the head – you may need a reference from him or her in the future.

Finally, I would like to wish you luck in the future, wherever, whatever and whoever you teach. As I said at the start of this book, you have made a wonderful choice of career. Try to look on the difficult times as a challenge and enjoy those indescribable moments of joy when you make a new discovery with a class, help a weak student to succeed, or when your children tell you just what you mean to them. It is a rare and very special job that can offer you all this and more.

Appendix One

Teaching jargon: A user's guide

Since you're becoming a teacher, I'd like to welcome you to the world of acronyms, abbreviations and complicated sounding jargon. Without this guide, a lot of the profession will be indecipherable to the 'normal' person (and perhaps that is partly the idea). This page gives you a brief run down of some of the key jargon and terminology that you will run into in your first year as a teacher.

A level	Advanced level
AS level	Advanced Subsidiary level
ATL	Association of Teachers and Lecturers
ADD	Attention Deficit Disorder
ADHD	Attention Deficit Hyperactivity Disorder
AfL	Assessment for Learning
AR&R	Assessment, Recording & Reporting
BEd	Bachelor of Education
BT	Beginning Teacher
CPO	Child Protection Officer
CPD	Continuing Professional Development
CDG	Curriculum Development Group
DfE	Department for Education
EWO	Education Welfare Officer
EdPsyc	Educational Psychologist
EBD	Emotional / Behavioural Disorder
ESL	English as a Second Language
EAL	English as an Additional Language

EPD	Early Professional Development
GCSE	General Certificate of Secondary Education
GNVQ	General National Vocational Qualification
GRTP	Graduate and Registered Teacher Programmes
GTTR	Graduate Teacher Training Registry
HOD	Head of Department
HMCI	Her Majesty's Chief Inspector of Schools
HMI	Her Majesty's Inspector of Schools
ICT	Information and Communications Technology
IEP	Individual Education Plan
INSET	In Service Training
ITT	Initial Teacher Training
KS	Key Stage
LSA	Learning Support Assistant
LEA	Local Education Authority
MFL	Modern Foreign Languages
NASUWT	National Association of Schoolmasters/Union of Women Teachers
NLS	National Literacy Strategy
NNS	National Numeracy Strategy
NVQ	National Vocational Qualification
NUT	National Union of Teachers
NQT	Newly Qualified Teacher
OFSTED	Office for Standards in Education
PTA	Parent Teacher Association
PSHE	Personal, Social and Health Education
PGCE	Post Graduate Certificate in Education
PAT	Professional Association of Teachers
QTS	Qualified Teacher Status
RTP	Registered Teacher Programme
SAT	Statutory Assessment Tasks
SCITT	School Centred Initial Teacher Training
SEN	Special Educational Needs
SENCO	Special Educational Needs Co-ordinator
SLT	Senior Leadership Team
SMT	Senior Management Team
STRB	School Teachers' Review Body
SpLD	Specific Learning Difficulty

TTA	Teacher Training Agency
TA	Teaching Assistant
TES	The Times Educational Supplement

Appendix Two

Internet links

http://www.education.gov.uk/schools/careers/payandpensions/
teacherspayandconditionsdocument/a0064179/school-teachers-pay-and-
conditions-document–2011 – The School Teachers' Pay and Conditions
Document

http://education.gov.uk/schools/careers/payandpensions/a00201183/salary –
Salary scales explained

www.woodlands-junior.kent.sch.uk/ – A great site run by a junior school in
Kent, which has loads of ideas and resources.

www.tes.co.uk/staffroom – Forums for discussing all aspects of being a
teacher – a great place for online networking and finding ideas.

Index